ᴬ Place for Us

Compiler and Editor

Geoffrey Duncan

ISBN 0 85346 230 5
© The United Reformed Church, 2004

Compiled by Geoffrey Duncan

Published by
Granary Press
the imprint of The United Reformed Church
86 Tavistock Place, London WC1H 9RT

Produced by Communications and Editorial, Graphics Office

Printed by Healeys Printers, Unit 10, The Sterling Complex,
Farthing Road, Ipswich, Suffolk IP1 5AP

Contents

Dedication

A Place for Us is dedicated to my grand-daughter Asha Louise Patil.

It is my hope Asha, that you will always work for a society where everyone has a place. Then we shall have justice and peace.

Introduction

We have our dreams ...we have our hopes ... . Many people look forward to the time when we shall be an inclusive society where the church will play an important and informed role. A place where everyone will be welcome and included as a part of the community. Everyone must be there. Just imagine the diversity ... the creativity ... the skills ... sharing in each other's hopes and dreams and challenges.

A Place for Us started out in life over a conversation with Carol Rogers, the Secretary for Communications of the United Reformed Church when we talked about an anthology on bereavement. Bereavement in a wide sense, which would include loss of employment, the break-up of a marriage or the dissolution of a partnership, bullying in the playground and workplace, illness and shattered lives. Seeds were sown and then ideas began to grow. As people were approached for contributions the scenario became much wider. So, now we have a book which is enriched with the inclusion of material, amongst many others items, from people living with Alzheimer's Disease, Multiple Sclerosis, physical impairments experienced by people associated with John Grooms and people who are cared for by hostels for the homeless. The story of Medical Aid for Children in Iraq and the fact that two of our regular contributors wrote litanies to accompany this article is much appreciated.

Prayers and poems written by people who have experienced the death of a child will be helpful for ministers and people plunged into those situations. Likewise, the terrible tragedies which are inflicted on people through death and injury on the roads. The plight of people who live in very difficult circumstances in developing nations; the sheer resourcefulness of these women, men and young people and the ways in which they overcome difficulties receive a focus. Then there are writings with much hope and light for the future in the chapter, Travel Toward the Dawn. There is always hope if only we will look for it and often where we do not expect to find it. Wonderful people, in many different places are waiting to be accepted and lived alongside.

Please dip in ... use the material ... be very thankful, for all the people who provide the encouragement we need.

It has been a pleasure to work with Carol Rogers once again, especially as she always finds time to listen and talk through the creative ideas. Also, my thanks to Sara Foyle for her time and energy in producing the book in very good time. Contributors deserve a special word of thanks and as ever I am very grateful to the friends who provide the material. There are always my many friends and colleagues in the United Reformed Church and in ecumenical circles who willingly respond to yet another request for prayers ... for litanies ... for stories ...and so life goes on.

Geoff Duncan
February 2004.

To Become More Aware

In the Depths of Silence

In the depths of silence no words are needed.
No language required.
In the depths of silence we are called to
Listen.

Source Unknown

Sounds of Silence

In the 'long boring kind' of silence
We say 'Be there, God'
In the 'angry and frustrating kinds' of silence
We say 'Help us, God'
In the 'quiet thinking kind' of silence
We say 'Think with us, God'
In the 'don't know how or what to say' kind of silence
We say 'Open us, God'
In the 'humming bees and singing birds' kind of silence
We say 'Thank you, God'.

Hannah Warwicker and Janet Lees
England

Birth Brings a Promise of New Life Awaking

Birth brings a promise of new life awaking,
Dawning of hope through a child's open eyes,
Uncharted future is there for the making,
Challenge and change in a baby's first cries.

Every new life changes those who are around it
Making demands of commitment and care.
Calling for love to enfold and surround it,
Reshaping patterns by claiming a share.

Jesus the new-born crossed time's moving stages
Changing their course by the act of his birth,
Translating God from the mystery of ages,
Rooting our faith by his presence on earth.

Wonder and worship were waiting to greet him,
Love and devotion were to his command,
Life as transformed for the ones sent to meet him,
Touching their God in a child's outstretched hand.

Birth gives a promise of new life awaking.
Jesus the new-born calls us to new birth.
All that he promised is ours for the taking
When our commitment brings God down to earth.

Tune: 11.10.11.10
Marjorie Dobson
England

Children of God

Child of God, you came to Bethlehem,
born into poverty and vulnerable
in a city under occupation ...
You came -
and innocent children were slaughtered
at the command of a king
who saw you as a threat to his security.

Children of God, living in Bethlehem,
forced into poverty and vulnerable
in a city under occupation ...
He comes –
where innocents are slaughtered
in the interest of security ...
sharing the pain.

Wendy Ross-Barker
England

Light in Darkness

Light of Christ, enter into the darkness
        of oppression and humiliation
With your warming glow.
Fragile and vulnerable, as when you came
To a new-born manger.

Light of Christ, enter into the darkness
        of indifference and ignorance
With your startling brilliance.
Bold and challenging as when you confronted injustice
        with the powerful weakness of self-giving love.

Wendy Ross-Barker
England

Love was Born

So Love was born.
Love that was deep and real.
Love that was God,
God's love in the life of the world.

In these Christmas days, Lord,
Let your love live in our lives.

Then we shall know the joy you bring.
Then we shall know the love you share.
Then we shall see your love in others
And be surprised by unexpected signs of love.

In these Christmas days, Lord
Let your love live in our lives.

Then we shall be aware of those who cry out for love.
Then we shall open our hearts to the homeless and the hungry.
Then we shall know the need to break the chains
        of injustice and oppression.
And be ready to respond in words and actions
        which express the love you are.

In these Christmas days, Lord,
Let your love live in our lives.

Wendy Ross-Barker
England

A Prayer of a Desperate Parent

God of quiet and serenity,
Grant me patience as I tend to the morning chores
And the baby is screaming.
Encircle me with your calm as I try to concentrate on written work
And the baby is screaming.
Enfold me in your peace as I continue on the daily round
And the baby is screaming.

Zam Walker
Wales/Scotland

I'm A Kid

I'm a kid.

I like:
Playing computer games
(Mum says I should read more);
kicking the footie
(against our neighbour's wall – it winds her up);
chilling outside the newsagents with my mates
(the youth club is in a church);
sneaking a fag
(Dad says if he ever catches me ...)
watching South Park
(I'm not allowed);
listening to music
(LOUD);
looking at those pictures
(I've hidden the mag under the mattress).

I don't like:
Going to school
(it's boring);
going to church
(it's even more boring);
shopping with my parents
(they're embarrassing);
cleaning my room
(it looks like ground zero);
hearing Mum and Dad argue
(I get scared when they shout);
visiting Gran
(her house smells funny);
having anything to do with my sister
(she's mingeing).

'Youth today,' huh?
Tough!
I'm a role model –
You've got to become like me
To enter the kingdom of God

Kim Fabricius
Wales/USA

Grandchildren

With your eyes
the children of the world
are searching my face
asking me questions.

With your hands
the children of the world
hungry for bread
tug at my clothes.

With your trust
the children of the world
climb on my lap
seeking safe shelter.

With your arms
the children of the world
put theirs around me
pleading for justice.

Cecily Taylor
England

Inclusion

To be a part and not stand apart
To belong and not be isolated
To be accepted and not accommodated
To have friends and not just companions
To feel needed and not just a person with needs
To be a participant and not a spectator
To have responsibilities and not just enjoy rights
To have opportunities and not favours
Is to be really included

Dipti Bhatia
Dipti is blind and works with physically impaired children at Vidyasagar, Chennai,
south India

Excluded

Excluded from the garden
Excluded from the room
Distant voices sing and dance in a circle
Women meeting making connections
Breaking down barriers
Excluded from the room.

Where are the black women?
They should be here
Is our agenda not their agenda?
Is my agenda not my sisters'
It is easily dismissed
Excluded from the room.

Where are the women?
The blind, the deaf
The women in chairs
Women who hate deep flights of stairs
Physical barriers get in the way
Of spiritual intent
Excluded from the room.

Is my cross not your cross?
How can we meet?
Me with my wheels
You with your feet
How will we find out?
Excluded from the room.

Excluded from the well
It made a pleasant change
Usually they take me there
To put me in the water
Hoping for a miracle
To reverse the damage

Excluded from the garden
Excluded from the room

Jean Palmer
England

Mayan Prayer

I am praying
When I do not oppress the other gender.

I am praying when I do not discriminate people of a
different race.

I am praying
When I do not exploit another.
human being

I am praying
When I do not alter nature's balance.

I am praying
When I am truthful, just and sincere.

I am praying
When I enjoy the miracle of being alive.

Julio Quan
Source Unknown

Moment Catcher

I heard one time that a
man walked in the sand
with a Nazarene.
The Nazarene and the man
walked hand in hand.

Is one beach on one side of
the world the same as a beach
on the other side of the world,
'cos that's all in God's hand?
Everything is in the hand
Everything is in the hand
Whatever hand it may be
It remains to see
It is fair of face
After all it's up to us,
We are the human race.

Zico
Scotland
Via St George's Crypt, Leeds, England

Contact

What I say to you
may not be
what you hear;

what I see
will look different
through your window;

what I hear
may be upon a frequency
untuned by you;

but incredibly
penetrating eternity
we seem to sense
the brief impact
of communication.

Cecily Taylor
England

Sexuality

A palette of word-colours
reflecting patterned images of sexuality
shape and define who I am.

My world of childhood:
Brushed with soft petals of pinks, blues, lemons,
and stems of earthy brown,
coloured body-centred words that crawled and walked with me;
Reaching-out words which drew me into my parents' arms;
Relational-words interpreted 'love' and 'belonging and 'community'
The colours of sexuality lay hidden,
Cocooned within patterns of my childhood world.

The landscape of my teenage years,
like trees emerging out of morning mists,
embodied the string colours of reds, greens and indigo
mixed with the many shades-browns of a rain-soaked earth.
Body-centred words gazed back at me from mirrored images;
Exploring-words challenged sex, sensuality and self-image;
Reaching-out words defined taboos draped in shame and guilt;
Relational-words coloured the mysterious world of other sex.

The colours of sexuality were mere glimpses
emerging through my vibrant teenage landscape,
drawing me into patches of colour for which I still had no name.

Then came the colours of wife and mother.
Crimson-red body-centred words,
lavender hued sensual words,
emerald green relational words,
earth-brown exploring words,
purple patterned power words,
All interlaced and woven together,
A colour-washed quilt defining my journey
to own my sexuality as wholeness of self.

My palette of word-colours continues to journey with me.

No longer are they compartmentalised words,
No longer do they stand in clearly labelled containers.
Instead, they pour out in a glowing, rich cascade of colour
that defines who I am.
Through its luminous strands, the colours of sexuality dance and glow.
Sometimes they whirl with the colours of power,
Then twist and turn with the hues of creativity,
At times they sway in the arms of spirituality,
Many times they move to the rhythms of the sacred.

And receiving this dancing waterfall of colour
is the core of wholeness that glows within me;
the deep rich colours of intimacy.
the tender whispering of compassion and love
the crystal transparency of fragility and vulnerability,
all held within the wonder and mystery of the gift of sexuality.

My palette of colours connect me to the Divine,
The Creator and Birth-mother of an universe
sculptured as a sensual, connected community,
colour-washed in the brilliant colours of Life!

Ranjini Wickramaratne-Rebera
Sri Lanka/Australia

Dear Mum

How many times have I heard you say
that nothing would surprise you?
You were always tidying my room
ferreting out my misplaced meals;
the cold plate of curry
wedged under the bed,
the half eaten sandwiches in the drawer,
the empty vodka bottles.
For years I have been eating alone
finiking food
retreating into the comfort of sleep.
You always knew exactly where to look
between the sheets
for the sharp kitchen knife.
So why, when you found the letter
Dear Mum, did you cry?

Elizabeth Cambridge
England

This Is the Room

This is the room where you come to confess,
we share the comfort of the old settee.
Nothing you say will make me love you less.

Here you herded dragons and played princess,
and twisted tinsel on the Christmas tree.
This is the room where you come to confess

the place you built Lego, learnt to play chess,
the room where we planned every birthday tea.
Nothing you say will make me love you less.

At nineteen you find a need to express
your feelings, with which I may not agree.
This is the room you come to confess.

You tell me what I already can guess,
That you are gay, but did not choose to be.
Nothing you say will make me love you less.

I search for soft words to ease our distress
grieving for the girl who sits beside me.
This is the room where you come to confess.
Nothing you say will make me love you less.

Elizabeth Cambridge
England

All Are Welcome

Our notice board says 'all are welcome',
Of course, we're a friendly church
We'd not like it if anyone said otherwise!

Are we?
Our Bible says all are created in the image of God
We say, 'lovely to see you',

And yet, and yet we prejudge.

Is that man, introducing his partner Peter, welcome?
Is that single woman with her daughter welcome?
He's just come from prison and he expects a welcome?
And that refugee who is so lost?
And that group of youths just hanging around the door?

All are welcome including us with our prejudice and partiality!
Thanks be to God whose nature is welcome.

John Ll Humphreys
Wales/Scotland

The Stranger

'Welcome', he said
Averted eyes belying smile
'You'll find we are a friendly lot
We believe in knowing
      Who is who – what is what,
You seem a decent person – one of us
Of course' – he said – 'we proceed with caution
Can't be too careful – must decide
      Who is nice – who is not.
There, labels are useful
      Indeed I'd say priceless.'
Labels?
'Of course, save face, save time, save mistakes',
Labels?
'Yes –
strange, different,
    queer, gay,
        black, dubious parentage,
            lower class, uneducated, ignorant,
feeble-minded, fat, female,
      foreign, mis-conceived,
         diseased, deformed,

        thick, ill-mannered,
            hoofed and horned ...

Hoofed and horned?
'Labels, as I say keep the wheels and wings
Of rejects, seconds, thirds, fourths and fifths,
And similar folk, clamped and clipped.'
Labels, well-crafted, made to last
     (economical too)
Pre-formed from prejudice,
Re-cycled malice does for glue,
There is no choice – we decide
Though long ago, there was one
Who chose to bear the label servant
Not only that – but change his nature
Give up his God's sonship status
Becoming merely mortal-poor vulnerable fool,
He was, of course,
Despised, rejected, spat upon, and rightly so,
(Can't have you doing that, old son!)
We put him in his place, nailed him in fact
And labelled him –
Jesus of Nazareth, king of the Jews,
Holed him, and that footloose tribe, in one!
Where is he now?
'Dunno, don't care,'
He turned aside, a solitary soul, disconsolate
Deaf to the sound I heard
A million, million voices rang
A glorious company, as one
On bended knees, on dancing feet
Sang praises to their living Lord
and journeyed God-ward in love's wake.

Margaret Herbert
England

Bosom Friend

Today you came over to dinner for the first time
You not only came, you forgot your state and came
Usually women don't forget that tradition of inequality
But you came with a mind as large as the sky to my pocket size house
I thought you had ripped out all those caste things
You came bridging that chasm that divides us
Truly, friend, I was really happy
With the naïve devotion of Shabari I arranged the food on your plate
But the moment you looked at the plate, your face changed

With a little smirk you said 'Oh my – do you serve chutney-koshimbir that way?'
You still don't know how to serve food
Truly, you folk will never improve
I was ashamed, really ashamed
My hand which had just touched the sky was knocked down.

Hira Bandsode
India

Poem

Each day I roam
Because I have no home
I'm desolate and lonely
I have no money
'Cause I have no job
and I'd love to live somewhere homely.

People think I am just a drop-out
Because I sleep rough and don't look clean
But when one gets as low as me
Having a job, a comfortable home is just a dream.

When things go wrong in the family home
And the only answer is to leave
Or your parents put you out 'cause they've had enough
What can you do but walk the streets unclean.

Some of us give up after a while
And just look forward to our dole
But some of us do try to change things
We're not all of us bad on the whole.

Teresa Larkman
Via Nightstop, Shipley, England

For St Botolph's – Aldgate – London

While we condemn their wickedness,
The hungry and the hunted,
The homeless and oppressed
Praise God for their compassion,
As they are fed and dressed.

For God, or for humanity?
The thirsty and the wretched,
The addicted and the poor
Find in their generosity
An ever open door.

How do we weigh alternatives,
Closed handed and closed-minded?
The 'righteous' and the 'just'
Thank God we are not like them
Who will return to dust.

Can we still judge their 'sinfulness':
The wasting and the wasted,
The dying; can we dare?
And for me, a scarlet ribbon:
Scarlet ribbons for their care.

Paul Friett
England

Post-modern Case History

They met at the Council's Amenity Tip
and furnished their home from many a skip.
Aware that they'd left it rather late
and were both beyond their sell-by date,
they reckoned they'd make it with minimal scars
though he was from Venus and she was from Mars;
but their beautiful love which had seemed so unfadeable
after a while was biodegradable.

Cecily Taylor
England

N.F.A.
(based on an actual incident)

Here John Smith lies,
laid out in style.
He was a lonely man,
nobody left to cry.
John Smith is dead, found in a railway carriage,
no fixed abode.

Euston Station, platform five,
is no place to die;
he made the trains run late,
but nobody knew why.
John Smith is dead in a London terminus,
no fixed abode.

Brush his hair, comb his beard,
give him a little care,
ten pence was in his pocket,
though he had not paid the fare.
John Smith is dead near the left luggage,
no fixed abode.

Card in a welfare cabinet,
now we can all forget
after a final priestly prayer
speeds him off with no regrets
John Smith is dead, blown where the wind may wish
no fixed abode.

Colin Ferguson
England

Where is Justice?

To be disabled,
to be a woman
and to be a dark-skinned Indian
is to be trebly disadvantaged
and discriminated against
in our Malaysian society;
so where is justice?

A Malaysian Woman

Prayers for Trade Unions

Creating and Loving God
You call us to work
With you and with one another
To create a world
Where justice and love are real
For everyone and every person can know
Joy in their work
Comfort in their rest
And peace in their community.

But we have worked only for ourselves
And refused to hear your call
And turned away from one another
So that work is drudgery and exploitation
People have forgotten how to rest
And live in isolation

Forgive us, merciful god
And show us how to turn around
And follow your call to justice and love.

A Place for Us 21

We hold before you all those people
Who work through trades unions
To improve working conditions
Regulate working hours
And ensure that workers are properly paid.
Give them firmness of purpose
Clarity of vision and fine judgement
And help them negotiate with care
For the dignity and worth of all.

We hold before you all those people whose trade union work is dangerous
Who experience discrimination hatred and violence.
Give them courage and strength and hope
To continue the struggle
Until workers are properly valued
And wealth is justly shared show us all how to work and pray
For a world where every person can know
Joy in their work
Comfort in their rest
And peace in their community.
Amen

Heather Pencavel
England

Prayer for Regions and Nations

God of love you call us to find our identity
in relationship with you
and with one another.

> May our new regional and national structures
> Be the means to explore identity and relationship;
> May they be saved from tribalism and insularity
> And become channels of communication
> So that all may share in the experience of each
> And delight in the diversity of your creation.

God of justice and peace
You lead us to a vision of community
Based on mutual care
You call us to build structures which support the weak
And enable the just sharing of resources

> May regional chambers and national assemblies
> Be forums for the voice of all the people
> where the vision of justice and peace is shared;
> may their members be saved from greed and self-seeking

and make decisions by which the poorest will benefit
so that everyone can live in mutual trust and respect,
belonging to one another.

God of all creation
You inspire us to new efforts
In making and doing and inventing
In careful research and daring development
In engineering, science and technology;
In new exploits new forms of art and music, dance and drama,
So that we can enjoy our efforts and achievements
And be the people you made us to be.

May our development agencies
Work to ring real wealth to region and nation
So that there is enough good work for all;
May they enable people to live rich and balanced lives
And grow in understanding and experience
Of what it is to be fully human

Through Jesus Christ,
Who shared the life of a human community
and lived and died for the whole world.
Amen

Heather Pencavel
England

Listening God

Listening God
Listen to the voices of working people
who have seen new technology replace traditional crafts
who know what it is like to watch a community die
and be powerless.

Listen to the voices that don't know what to say
because everything goes on changing so fast
and the new jobs need new skills, a new kind of people
and flexibility has taken over from loyalty.

Listen to the boys who don't know how to be men
because even that has changed and it is hard
to earn enough to live today, to plan for tomorrow.

Listening God
you speak to humankind with unchanging love.
Show us how to bring new life to communities and people
to learn new ways of sharing both wealth and poverty,
new ways of working to serve one another,
new ways of being human,
as you did in Jesus, who is your Word to us.
Amen

Heather Pencavel
England

Where is God Today?

Where were you at eleven this morning, God?
Some people in the meeting were very angry
and some people were not telling the truth
some didn't know the truth of the matter
and some were afraid to speak out
afraid for their jobs, their prospects in the company
and I sat there and tried (it was important)
to do the best I could, give it all I had.
                              Where were you, God?

Where were you at three a.m. today, God?
We worked our guts out in the heat and noise
the safety locks undone to speed things up
not enough of us on shift to do things right
and two of us had worked the last shift too –
too tired to react quick when things go wrong.
We got through somehow, clocked off at six o'clock,
home through the waking streets in weariness.
                              Where were you, God?

Where were you at two this afternoon, God?
That's when they told me that I had to go.
It was, they said, 'a matter of regret –
out of their hands, a question of necessity,
early retirement, time to re-assess,
to downshift, look for other opportunities ...'
I only heard the sound of twenty years
of faithful effort flushed away like dirt –
                              Where were you, God?

My child, where you were there I was, God says.
I know too well
the struggle for justice
the back-breaking toil
rejection and despair –
in all of these I stand with you,
for I am with you always till the end of time.

God of the broken reed, the flickering wick,.
Christ of the bitter cross,
Spirit whose living flame kindles new life,
in all our work you live and breathe
and make again
a covenant of your redeeming grace
that calls us partners in creation.
all that we are and do we offer you
and join with gladness in your work in the world,
through Jesus Christ our Lord,
Amen.

Heather Pencavel
England

Today Tomorrow

Gone are the days when my memory was great
And my spelling was a hundred percent.
Writing and reading, cooking and cleaning
And managing the money I spent.

Today, tomorrow, when will it be
When this disease takes over me
Will it be Summer, Autumn or Spring
Shall I be forced to give in.

Sometimes I wonder, each day I awake
How much more dead cells will it take
It brings so much worry, so much stress
Why my mind is in so much mess.

So I'll think of today
Although tomorrow must come.
I must always stay positive and strong.

Margaret Alford
England
Via Alzheimer's Society/Living with Dementia Project

A Blessing for Someone Living with Alzheimer's

Lord, we ask your blessing on this confused mind.
You know that the experiences and knowledge of a lifetime
      are locked away inside a complicated mechanism to which
      this disease has inappropriate keys.

Keep this troubled one safe in confusion,
happy in forgetfulness,
aware in times of lucidity
and secure in the environment of constant care.

When there is fear and anger, surround ... with your peace.
When despair strokes, give her/him your glimmer of hope.
When there seems to be no response, probe deep into the apparent
      emptiness of the mind with the reassurance of your love.

And when everything seems hopeless and this disease has full
      control, we commit her/him to your eternal compassion and care.

Marjorie Dobson
England

Dancing Man

(Written for a colleague in Boston, Massachusetts whose father was last seen entering the World Trade Centre on 11 September 2001)

Dancing Man, dancing slow
Just wishing to let you know
That tears are in his eyes for you.

Praying man, praying long
And hard, for this world, so wrong,
For tears are in God's eyes too.

Loving man, loving friend,
Life might, but love has no end,
For God's Love is in his heart.

Dancing man, loving friend,
Praying for the pain to end
Or, for now, healing to start.

Paul Friett
England

Insight

I've seen the light, revealing church dysfunction.
The truth, children meeting parental needs.
The way, an exodus beyond the slavery.
The key, that unlocks the blockages.
The door, that opens towards opportunity.
The gate, an opening to reveal green pastures.
The life, deathly monotony has lost its hold.
The resurrection, casting off the shroud of death.
The hope, certainty of new horizons.
The vine, laughter is in evidence.
The glory, crowning days of life.

Frances Ballantyne
England

Discovering Respect for One Another

Within a minute of arrival, the children were there, milling around, fascinated. 'You must be famous!' 'I've seen you on TV!' Neither of which are true but the only meaningful frame of reference to them for a foreigner to be here. A place where foreigners never come, and, more darkly, 'Where are your bodyguards?'

This is the 'city' of Bolivar a slum perched on the hills around Bogotá. It is a place of refuge for thousands of people with either economic need or the failure of security driving them in from the country.

The irony is that no one comes here if they can avoid it. The school standing at one end of a central square – a rough, flattened place of compacted mud and tufted grass – has not seen a teacher for years. Army conscripts sometimes come, play basketball with the children, teach them songs, and go. At the church opposite, no one can tell me its denomination. They have not seen a pastor or a priest. The building is shut up, its veranda a meeting place, its paint peeling.

It is abandoned because it is poor. It is abandoned because it is violent – public space is crime ridden while in private space domestic violence is prevalent.

I had come to visit a 'trust bank'. A group of women who had come together for mutual support, to develop their mutual savings and to borrow money to start or develop a small enterprise.

One of the group, Luiz, took me to her small shop – a stall on the side of her house where she sold basic groceries. I asked to me a familiar question: 'Can you tell me what difference the loan has made to your life?' Waiting in the pause, playing through my mind, the familiar pattern of answers about enabling a family to keep its children in school, improving access to medicines, a new roof on one's home or a stable, concrete floor.

But, 'My husband no longer beats me,' came the surprising reply. 'No,' echoed the husband, 'I no longer beat her!' Taken aback by this candour, I asked, 'Why?'

'Because now I know that her business makes money, rather than losing it,' answered the husband, 'the strain of making ends meet has lessened.' 'I have changed,' answered Luiz, 'I contribute to the family and we have rediscovered our respect for one another. We lost this when we moved from the country – together with everything else.'

The women's mutual support and their changing circumstances, of hope as much as of material, brought about by acquiring a degree of economic independence, had changed the dynamics in this family from fragmentation, an alienating separateness, to a renewed cohesion, a common purpose. It was a story repeated throughout my visit, kept short so as not to draw attention to myself, but visits made every day by the staff of ADEMCOL, the agency responsible for organising the trust bank.

Young women themselves, they brave the uncertainties of this place to be catalysts of 'trust' and foster the rebirth of hope, slowly nurturing a renewed sense of community in a place bereft of many of community's traditional focuses. It is bravery and a commitment that is a witness to their faith, and a challenge to ones own.

Nicholas Colloff
England

Stan

Stan was a miner. When I knew him, though
He's changed his status thirty years before
To that of mental patient. Stanley often spoke to me
About his special childhood in a nearby town
Or rather village, Gorbar village, as he said,
That's where I went to church, singing on Sundays,
Mornings and evenings, Book of Common Prayer,
Stan grinned at me, 'I'll take you back', I said
He grinned again, pleased at the thought. I never
Mentioned it again, although some years passed by
And Stanley never held me to my word.

So when one Autumn afternoon, I stopped the van
Opened the door and said, 'Come on, hop in,
I'm taking you to Gorbar like we said, hop in',
I thought he might be startled and say 'no'
But Stan just grinned and so away we went …

At Gorbar village church our way was blocked
By mourners and a hearse: and when she heard
Just who we were and why we'd come, the Verger there
Seeing at once the better part of valour
Bundled us out and sent us on our way
Politely. Stanley just grinned. He'd seen the church, he said
Next we called on Stan's young niece. 'Hello', she said
'How nice to see you, Uncle, it's been years. I've made
Some ginger cake. And this is Debs'. Stanley squatted down
Before the electric fire; for half an hour he stayed
Playing with the little girl, then 'Time to go', he said.

Back at the van and on again. Now came the hardest part
'I want to see my eldest brother now', he said. 'I mean
The one who shut me up for all this time' …
I looked at Stanley and he grinned at me. 'You know
The way, Stan?' It's almost thirty years. What if …
Stan grinned. 'Go right … left … right,' he said
Right at these bollards, then the left hand road
Now down the hill and up. I couldn't help but think
We were both lost. Then Stan said, 'Stop!'
'Stop here, that's right, it's over there.' I looked around
One of these places, new but seeming old, where roads
Turn inwards on themselves and move in circles
Towards the centre, so you don't so much arrive
As are confronted. 'Look, here we are. It's number 397
You go, Roger. Tell them who it is.' Gritting my teeth
I climbed out of the van. 'Mr Slater, no you don't
know me. I've brought your brother along, he'd like
to see you.' He didn't move a muscle. 'Well,' he said
'I'm having my tea, see? You'd better bring him in, though.'
He looked at Stanley trying not to show he knew
Him. Stanley stared back and shook his hand, quite warmly
Though.
We got back in the van, 'left, left, right, right.' 'It's not much further now,'
Stan said and grinned 'hang on
We're nearly home.'

Roger Grainger
England

Stretch Out Your Hand

Endless time to stand and stare
Even tonight in the cold night air;
Stiffly, silently, watching her breath –
Minus possessions –
Save blankets for warmth
Plus a prized travel-chess.

Where's she heading?
As if you'd not guess;
Yes, she's but one
Of this world's homeless,
Totally oblivious of time,
Shabby, lonely, resigned.

Her cultured voice is no surprise
A bottle beside her – to idolise;
Standing, waiting – inwardly weeping
An ailing body that bears many a scar
So much for social justice
With every freedom – to frequent the bar!

Now – let me stretch out my hand to you
Be assured, times are changing
On the horizon of hope
The Holy Spirit's engaging
Her powers to renew –
With friends about to embrace; welcome; rescue;
Heralding peace as a dove – miraculously healing,
Steering away from the artificial and false
So this night in the open,
Please God, could well be your last
As each cardboard city collapses in ruins
A thing of the past!

Wendy Whitehead
England

What is God Worth?

What is God worth?
We have calculated the value of the life of human beings
        in compensation cases.
We have even calculated the value of a child
        based on what it costs to rear one;
            tens of thousands of pounds spent on nappies, school books, clothes
        and food.

And we compare values:
>   one American soldier worth more than one Kosovan Albanian;
>   the value of British love shown in flowers worth more
>   than a Chilean's health affected by pesticide exposure;
>   the loss of a marriage partner in a Soho bomb blast
>   worth more than half a gay relationship;
Human lives, costed, tied up in neat packages, measured.
But what value, really?

What is God worth?
>   God who made the Pleiades and Orion, who turns blackness into dawn and
>   darkens day into night;
>   God who forms the mountains, creates the wind, and dares to reveal thoughts
>   to us;
>   God who loved the world so much that the one and only Son was given in
>   order that whoever believes shall not perish but have eternal life;
God who gave the right to become children of God, co-heirs with Christ;
>   The One who chose us before the creation of the world to be holy
>   and blameless;
The One who marks us with a seal, the promised Holy Spirit;
God, the Alpha and the Omega, the First and the Last, the Beginning
>   and the End.

What is God worth?
An hour of your time on Sunday and 50p in the collection plate?

Jenny Spouge
England

Sunset

See the reds, the pink, the orange –
how incredibly they glow –
in the sky above the valley
where the burger bars now grow.

All the bored and busy people
hurrying to their Habitats,
never see the sunset glory
from their top floor tower block flats.

'Coronation Street' and 'Neighbours'
keep them busy after tea,
while outside the sunset's glory
blazes out with none to see.

Look above your Laura Ashley.
See the sky of gold and pink.
God with his eternal paintbox
just beyond your kitchen sink.

Marjorie Dobson
England

Water Is ...

Water is
    rain and gutters,
    hurricanes that bang shutters.
    'Cats and dogs' and thunderstorms;
    rain has got so many forms.

Water is
    ripples and waves,
    carving out cliffs, making dark caves.
    In and out across the shore;
    sea is water that can roar.

Water is
    from tap or well,
    precious treasure or stuff to sell.
    Clean, dirty, moving or still;
    water gives life or can kill.

Water is
    just H – 2 – O;
    molecule that can freeze or flow.
    Power for mills and engines too:
    I love water, how about you?

Hannah Warwicker and Janet Lees
England

Running Out of Food

Running Out of Food   – cupboards getting low on 'basics'

Running Out of Food   *– so scratch about in dried up earth*

Running Out of Food   – so do a 'big' shop

Running Out of Food   *– drought has ruined the harvest*

Running Out of Food   – fridge getting empty

Running Out of Food   *– no money to buy any more*

Running Out of Food   – so let's save ourselves the trouble
and go out for a meal

Running Out of Food   – *so walk for miles to see what can be found*

Running Out of Food   – but friends will do the shopping while I'm ill

Running Out of Food   – *no-one can shop while the curfew is imposed*

Running Out of Food   – so fill up the freezer

Running Out of Food   – *malnutrition is a certainty*

Running Out of Food   – so have a baking day

Running Out of Food   – *starvation and death*

Running Out of Food   – ...

Running Out of Food   – ...

Wendy Ross-Barker
England

Father Forgive

The hatred which divides nation from nation,
     race from race,
     class form class.

Father forgive.
The covetous desires of people and nations to possess what is not their own.

Father forgive.

The greed which exploits the labours of men and women and lays waste the earth

Father forgive.

Our envy of the welfare and happiness of others

Father forgive.

Our indifference to the plight of the homeless and refugees

Father forgive.

The lust which uses for ignoble ends the bodies of men, women and children.

Father forgive.

The pride which leads us to trust in others and not in God.

Father forgive.

Ecumenical Forum of European Christian Women

Report from the Front

The most painful battle
Is raging right here.
Do you hear the shots
Ringing down the phone line?
Do you hear my sobbing breath
As I struggle to win back
All the land I so needlessly yielded?

Diane D'Souza
south India/England

It Is High Time We Decided

Oh my people
Why all the loud cries
Why the guns and the bombs
Why destroy the land,
The innocent souls
Why the division
Oh my people.

Oh my people
When shall we unite?
When shall we decide 'we want peace'
Oh yes, it is high time we decided
Oh my people

Oh my people
It is very easy to cry and blame
It is very easy to talk of disunity,
In justice and oppression
It is very easy to sign peace agreements
It is very easy, easy, easy …
Oh my people.

Oh my people
Who is the enemy?
Who is to call off the war?
Who is to sow peace?
Who is to restore the dignity,
The hope and the lost love?
Oh my people.

It is high time we decided from our hearts.

Frances Phillips
Via Jesuit Refugee Service, Uganda

Missionary Encounters

When I got home from Church House the other night, in addition to all the junk mail that Chris gets (buy a new stethoscope and get a mystery gift absolutely free), there was one of those aggrieved notes from the postman complaining that he'd slogged all the way up the lane with a parcel for me only to find that I wasn't in.

Usually, Gordon (the postman) leaves parcels with one of my neighbours, or in extremity, with the children's pet, Kenny – a rabbit so savage that if you are not bearing fruit or vegetables in copious quantities, thievery is out of the question. But on this occasion everyone else was out too and Kenny was sulking because of pouring rain and losing a fight with Benny the guinea pig.

This meant that I had to go down to the parcel collection outpost of the Post Office to collect my Amazon order. Sounds easy but it's not. Said PO outpost is situated on a large roundabout with no parking anywhere. People cut across two lanes of traffic, stick the car on double yellow lines and sprint into the office hoping that (a) a Morrisons lorry does not mash your rear-end into metal porridge and (b) (worse) 'Helga' the traffic warden doesn't get you.

Helga – not her real name – is a redoubtable lady about four foot six inches tall and similarly wide. She cannot be reasoned with, argued with, wept in front of, cajoled or bought. The roundabout is her special territory and if you park there she will get you.

But I happen to know something about Helga. She is a creature of habit. At 11.00 she meets with another traffic warden and they sneak off for a cup of tea in a local café. For a brief period, it's open season on the roundabout.

So off I went. The only trouble was about twenty other people had had the same idea. There were so many hazard lights flashing it looked like a major pile up. I squeezed into a tiny tributary off the main roundabout and made a dash for the Post Office. There was a queue of agitated people, all keeping an uneasy eye on the window and hoping Helga would be deep in gossip or tempted by another currant bun.

Parcels are staffed by Jim. If you can't argue with Helga, you definitely can't rush Jim. Jim takes his time. If the phone rings, he answers it. If Jesus arrived to pick up his Amazon order he'd have to wait patiently in line until Jim was good and ready and if he didn't have the proper identification, then he wouldn't be getting his Inspector Morse videos that day, no sir.

Eventually it was my turn. I was feeling uneasy because in the distance out of the window, I could see Helga emerging from the town centre with her friend. Jim smiled 'Identification, please', he said, as if he'd never seen me before.

On this occasion I gave him my Church House pass which has my name and picture on it. He studied it for a minute. 'Board of Mission ... 'he mused. 'Is that like, to do with missionaries'. 'Yes,' I said, not wanting to start a complicated conversation.

'You know I was in the Merchant Navy?'

'Yes. You know I do, you've told me a hundred times.'

'Did I ever tell you once I rescued a missionary from death?'

'No' And I don't care, just give me the parcel!

Jim tucked my parcel comfortable under his arm. The phone rang but he ignored it. He told me a story of how, years ago, captaining a large ship, he came across a missionary struggling in a dinghy, trying to get between islands and overwhelmed by weather.

Jim rescued the man and took him in, half dead from exposure and gave him chicken soup because he'd been told it was 'the right thing to do'. He rescued the man's belongings and dried them out, including Bibles and religious literature that he had been trying to bring to the people of the islands. He saved his life.

Jim's eyes had gone rather dreamy and he was clutching my parcel harder than ever. I was vaguely aware of the restless shifting of people behind me and wondered if I was being told this story to brighten up Jim's otherwise dull day.

Suddenly, a few people gave up and ran for it. Helga was back but I was stuck. My heart sank, here I was about to get a ticket all because I'd been too soft to stop a dotty old bloke from telling me some fantasy rescue story.

I'd stopped listening. Jim gave me the parcel and I signed for it. But he had something else he wanted me to sign. I reached for it.

'No look', he said crossly, from somewhere under his counter, he'd taken out a very old piece of paper, battered and crushed, with old fashioned print that was barely legible. On it was the Lord's Prayer.

He said, quietly, 'He gave me that. And I keep it by me and I say it every day. Helps me get through, you know, in here.' He gave me a conspiratorial nod.

Helga came in and fixed me with a maniacal stare. 'Is that YOUR car?' she barked, pointing out of the window,.

'Yes' I said miserably. 'WELL MOVE IT!' she bawled.

I couldn't believe my luck.

Back at home, I reflected on the many layers that had come out of a stupid little trip to the Parcel Collection office. My Church House pass sparked it, and who would have thought of that?

That one word 'mission' had released the story of a powerful encounter in which it was the missionary who needed the help, compassion and care of others to do God's work. Without that chicken soup, God's messenger might not have survived.

Out of that encounter came a message,
A resource which sustained another in the years to come.

And as for me, I nearly missed it, I was in a hurry and was concerned about my own selfish well-being. I didn't want to hear the story and because my own concerns were paramount was ready to dismiss it.

Another few seconds and I would never have known about the Lord's Prayer and it's part in Jim's life.

If I had got the ticket I might not have cared. All I wanted was to walk in, get the parcel, walk, out go home. But if I call myself 'missionary', why do I not ask where else the encounter presents itself? What other Post office counters, supermarket checkouts, bank desks, market stalls have people with stories to tell about what God has done in their life?

How on earth do we create the space to hear them? How shall we hear?

Maybe, just maybe, Helga too has a story to tell, if not that, at least once, she allowed a motorist to get away with it. Why did that happen? If I go past the café at 10'clock, I am resolved to find out.

Anne Richards
England

In Memory of All the Women

In memory of all the women
who have struggled against poverty,
hidden in statistics
yet fighting for food and survival.
We break our silence:
and raise our voices in anger and hope.

In memory of all the women
who have known suffering and death,
facing their pain
with a courage born of their own dignity'
We break our silence:
and raise our voices in anger and hope.

In memory of all the women
who have cared for others,
offering the precious gift of themselves
In love and service.

We break our silence:
and raise our voices in anger and hope.

In memory of all the women
who have celebrated life in word
and image and song,
creating meaning and transforming vision
by the power of their art.
We break our silence:
and raise our voices in anger and hope.

In memory of all the women
who have proclaimed truth and freedom,
declaring the coming of justice
in their words and actions.
We break our silence:
and raise our voices in anger and hope.

Jan Berry
England

Modest yet Mutinous, Striving for Justice

Modest yet mutinous, striving for justice,
seeking to comfort our neighbours who fell;
we were downtrodden, but now not derided
walking Christ's path, bringing light to life's hell.

Hell is were love is denied or distorted,
hell is next door or is right in this place,
hell is not future but bound to the present,
hell is the vacuum that cries for God's grace.

Grace is the offering of love to a neighbour,
grace is a selfless expression of care,
grace will flow freely when justice is founded,
grace is the gift that we all seek to share.

11.10.11.10
Andrew Pratt
England

Confession on the Road

For the journey of the planets, the thread of life;
We praise you, God.
For the journey from Nazareth to Jerusalem, the steps of life;
We praise you, God.
For the journey outwards and inwards, the breath of life;
We praise you, God.
For the times we sent the planet off course;
Lord, have mercy
For the stumbling blocks we put on the road to peace;
Christ, have mercy
For the times we chose death over life;
Lord, have mercy

Silence

People of the way, listen to these life-giving words;

'Your faith has saved you:
Go in peace'.

Thank you God.

Janet Lees
England

Discovering Ourselves

A Personal Creed

It is my belief to wonder,
To look closely, listen intently,
Strive purposefully, persuade gently,
To count my blessings thankfully
And to experience joy. And though
I question constantly,
I will seek diligently,
Say my prayers fervently
And wait patiently
For the answers.

Celia Snaith
England

You Are Very Special

This piece has been read at various dedication services for children

In all the world there is nobody, nobody like you.
Since the beginning of time there has never been
        another person like you.
Nobody has your smile, your eyes, your hands, your hair.
Nobody owns your handwriting, your voice.
You're special.

Nobody can paint your brush strokes.
Nobody has your taste for food, or music, or dance, or art.
Nobody in the universe sees things as you do.
In all time there has never been anyone who laughs
        in exactly your way,
        and what makes you laugh, or cry, or think
        may have a totally different response in another.
So you're special.

You're different from any other person who
        has ever lived in the history of the universe.
You are the only one in the whole creation
        who has your particular set of abilities.
There is always someone who is better at one thing or another.
Every person is your superior in at least one way.
Nobody in the universe can reach the quality of the combination
        of your talents, your feelings.
Like a roomful of musical instruments some might excel

in one way or another
but nobody can match the symphonic sound
when all are played together,
Your symphony.
Through all eternity no-one will ever walk, talk,
think or do exactly like you.
You're special.

You're rare and in all rarity there is enormous value.
And because of your great value the need for you
to imitate anyone else is absolutely wrong.
You're special and it is no accident that you are.

Please realise that God made you for a special purpose.
He has a job for you to do that nobody else can do as well as you.
Out of the billions of applicants only one is qualified.
Only one has the unique and right combination of what it takes
and that one is you.
You're special.

Source Unknown

Through All the Changing Scenes ...

Five! Alive! Now see me go!
Splash through raindrops, stomp through snow.
Life's for living – finding out
what my world is all about.

Twenty-five! My path is clear.
I know where I'll be next year.
Future perfect. Partner picked.
Look out life! I've got you licked.

Forty-five! Safe and secure.
No longer brash and immature.
Healthy, happy, unconcerned.
I'm enjoying what I've earned.

Sixty-five! Retired at last!
Life was getting far too fast!
Now my time is all my own –
can't believe how fast it's flown.

Eighty-five! Can this be me?
My mirror tells me what you see.
My secret life the glass will hide –
I'm still a five-year-old inside!

Marjorie Dobson
England

I Am Not Alone

I stand in wonder and behold
Visions of faith, insights of love
Beauty I never sowed unfold
Somehow there is in me yet more
Than I myself might settle for
I am not alone.

There is no limit to what
Prayer can bring
To whom the soul loves well
Refreshment from a hidden spring
I am not alone.

Walking in the sunlight
I catch at times the reflecting
Glisten of myself
I know I am not alone
God is always with me
I am, not alone.

Tiny Powell
England

Open To Me

Open to me, my brother.
I have knocked at your door,
I have appealed to your heart,
to have a bed,
to have a little fire to warm me.
Open to me, my sister.
Why do you ask me
if I am African,
or Asian,
or European?
I am not black,
nor is my skin red;
I am not oriental,
nor white.
I am simply a man.
I am simply a woman.
Open to me,
Open your door to me.
For I am like you,
A stranger of all times,
under every sky.
A man, a woman,
like you.

Rene Philombe
Cameroons

Retirement

Now I am retired, who am I?

Once I had status,
the satisfaction of a job well done.
Colleagues formed a colony,
and we were comfortable in our world.
The days were busy,
too much so, at times;
but there was pattern, structure
and a motive to the day.

Now that sense of purpose is no more.
No reason why anyone should consult me,
talk to me,
or ask me how the day has gone.

I'm lost –
and this strange world of nothingness
stretches before me,
except for eating and sleeping and being entertained.
Knowledge, skills, experience –
All in the past.

Unless you can find a new use for them, Lord?

Marjorie Dobson
England

Mothering God

Mothering God,
there are times when we need to nestle into your arms
as a child needing comfort.
Nothing else can soothe us,
but the knowledge that you know and care about us.
Help us in our times of unease, or distress
and reassure us with your love.

We pray for all those who need you in this way.
Open our eyes to all those who seek for solace
as they search for you.
Help us to help them
to find their way into your love.

Marjorie Dobson
England

An Affirmation of Inclusiveness

I believe in the divine mystery that is beyond all definition
yet reflected in a thousand images.

I believe in the expanding and recycling processes of nature
and of the cosmos as a whole, epitomised in the birth, life, death and
resurrection of Jesus Christ.

I believe in the energy of spirit in all its creative, destructive
and empowering activities.

I believe that the journey of forgiveness can free people from the
power of past hurts.

I believe that everything is interconnected and interwoven and
that in this living this awareness lies the fullness of life.

I believe in the experience of eternity that comes through silence,
wonder and love to transform the present moment.

I believe in my own value as a child of God and seek to see God in
all other human beings.

I accept my role as a co-worker with God in the processes of the
evolving Universe
and determine to work for justice, peace and reverence for the whole
of creation.

This is my resolve and I will seek to accomplish this through co-operation.
With all who share these goals; in the strength of imagination
compassion
and wonder.

W L Wallace
Aotearoa New Zealand

I Know a Boy

I know a boy quiet as mischief
loud as cymbals
Broad as dawn his smiling

If you ask him where he is rowing
over the grass – there is no knowing
the other side of the sun.

I know a boy fast as spacemen
slow as treacle
sure as trees his climbing.

If you ask him when all his playing
comes to an end – there is no saying,
the day would never be done.

I know a boy full as summer
tired as yawning
deep as love his sleeping.

Cecily Taylor
England

When I Was Very Young

When I was very young
I became frightened
When I saw people
Who looked different,
Spoke differently,
Walked differently,
Then when I took
My first service
At a psychopaedic home
I remembered
My past fears
And again became
Discomforted.
But soon I discovered
Warm hearts behind unusual faces
And learning to avoid their spittle,
Rejoiced in the warmth of their hugs
And the delight of their welcome.
It was indeed a world devoid of
Pretence, superficiality
Or reserve.

In them I saw what we were all meant to be
Delightful, playful, loving creatures,
It was then that I realised
That a misshapen mind or heart
Is a far worse disability
Than any unusual features
Of face, gesture or speech.

W L Wallace
Aotearoa New Zealand

Detention

My school friends disappear with joyful din
Towards the tennis courts, their thoughts on play,
But I, detained indoors, can't see where May
Illumines all the chestnut trees. So in
This ink-bespattered classroom hand cups chin
Where shafts of sun-split chalk mockingly stray,
While I learn lines of verse. I must obey
That sternest voice to expiate my sin.

But the dishevelled schoolroom turns for me
Into enchanted Darien; intent
I watch Horatio's proud bravery,
Hear clashing of blade on blade as the air is rent;
It is as well the teacher cannot see
Me smile to think she counts it punishment.

Cecily Taylor
England

The Blessing of the Bizarre

I had a weekly appointment at a high school. I would arrive just as the
pupils were leaving for the day. The school provided something of an
alternative education for young people who have had difficulty settling
at one of the more traditional schools. There is no school uniform.
The appearance of these young people was something of a shock!
The girls, in particular, wear astonishing ensembles: some with long,
usually black skirts to the floor, others wearing miniskirts, tights and
boots; often underwear would be worn on the outside. Boys and girls
have hair either long and dyed bright colours or shaven off all together.
Almost everyone is decorated with rings: pierced through ears, nostrils,
eyebrows, lips, navel, sometimes tongue! As the weeks passed, however,
I began to see these youngsters differently.
I got to know some of them. I discovered they are on the whole pleasant
and polite, sometimes happy, sometimes sad like everyone in their age
group. I began to delight in the imagination and flair revealed in the
way they dress. I rejoiced in their freedom from slavery to the dress
conventions which, though petty, are strong in the community.
The vision of the Pharisees persists and oppresses yet. We can rejoice in
the blessing of God's love for the individuality of each and every person.

John Hunt
Aotearoa New Zealand

Hear Me, Dear Lord

Hear me, dear Lord, in this time of sorrow,
for even if I turn from you today,
I need to know your love is there tomorrow
and new hope still can brighten up my way.

Forgive me, Lord if in the tears of sadness
my anger makes me take your name in vain
and life seems for a while to have no gladness
while I refuse to let you share my pain.

Hold me, dear Lord, in the surrounding darkness,
help me in faith to know what you have said,
that even in death's unremitting starkness,
the son of man has risen from the dead.

So take this life that's left with its misgivings
And from the past's remains create anew
A hope that finds in you a way of loving,
A love that offers all it has to you.

Tune: Intercessor
Colin Ferguson
England

Thirst

To all things there is a season:

a time to give out
a time to take in
a time of being drained
a time for replenishing
a time to say yes eagerly
a time to say no wisely;
a time to hold on
and a time to let go.

I have come to the time of drinking in –
the thirst is great and terrible.
Time I need to drink in sunsets,
to wait like a blackbird
listening for worms.

Time I need to hear
what the leaves have to tell me,
and time to sleep and sleep.

Time to hug to me sanity,
time to hold silence like a promise
in my two cupped hands.

Time to think with God
alone in some wilderness of solitude,
and then – with love returning
then only, to share.

Cecily Taylor
England

Who Am I? (1)

I am a woman, I am a Filipino
     I am alive, I am struggling
          I am hoping

I am created in the image of God
     Just like all other people in the world;
I am a person with worth and dignity;
I am a thinking person, a feeling person, a doing person.

I am the small I am that stands before the big I AM.
I am worker who is constantly challenged
     and faced with the needs of the church and society in Asia
     and in the global community.

I am angered by the structures and powers
     that create all forms of oppression, exploitation and degradation.

I am witness to the moans, tears, banners and clenched fists of my people.

I can hear their liberating songs, their hopeful prayers and
     decisive march toward justice and freedom.

I believe that all of us – women and men
     young and old, Christian and non-Christian
     are called upon to do responsible action:
     to be concerned , to be involved
     NOW!

I am hoping, I am struggling, I am alive.
     I am Filipino, I am a woman

Elizabeth Tapia
Philippines

Who Am I? (2)

From being a young child
I've never known
Bonding and attachment
My seeds are now sown

I'm a person, a human I feel
Emotion and pain
I want to be someone
To feel alive again

Discovering Ourselves

I want to be safe
To feel loved and secure
I want to be wanted, I'm a person
An innocent child, still pure

I hide my pain, my fear
I try so hard to be strong, sometimes I can't shed a tear
I feel my sadness will never end
I want to be part of a family, with love and some friends

I just don't understand
Why my life has to be like this
I know we all suffer heartache and pain
I never expected it to be total bliss

Each time I conquer a battle
Of pain and emptiness
The harder I try
The more I face loneliness

You can guide me or shout at me
I don't really care
I just need to know
You will always be there

Just tell me and show me
When I've done something wrong
I'll understand your discipline
It will make me feel strong

It's when there is no one
To help me, to guide me, to care
I feel I'm walking in limbo
I need to feel I can share

I want to be someone
I want to feel a part
I need to focus on life
I need a fresh start

If somebody wants me
I will be so happy and free
I will be the best person in the world
You will be so proud of me

Please give me a chance
All I need is a little help
I don't want to live when I feel
Just a shadow of myself

Ann Bedingfield
Via Nightstop, Shipley, England

Faith Encounter

As God made you,
God made me
Though differently
For life's purposes
Today; tomorrow.
Your thought forms,
Visions, lifestyles,
Venues for worship;
Ways into God
All have much to teach
In the common quest of each.

Let me learn from you,
You from me –
Reaching out together
For that healing touch;
Daily journeying on
Toward life's goal
United in holy pilgrimage.

Brave hearts –
Building, reconciling,
Empowering by God's spirit
Continue in joyous faith
Toward the Celebration Day
When all God's world, we pray,
Is born anew –
At one in speech and sight
In radiant resurrection light.

Wendy Whitehead
England

I Can Sing Your Goodness

Blessed are you, O Lord our God, King of the universe
Who has made me a woman,
Who has given me a unique understanding of your design
And purpose in creation, who is not to be coveted,
Who has created me with the potential to share
The same suspense of secret expectation,
Patient waiting in hope, bearing in love,
Total selfless involvement in bringing new life to birth,
That is yours,
That, with Mary
I can sing your goodness,
Become a vessel of creative love and human hope,
Know the pain and pleasure of giving birth,
Rest in deep satisfaction, folding new life in my arms,
Though awestruck and a little fearful at the trust that is placed in me,
Be bolstered by your cradling care,
And might, rejoicing, keep this knowledge close
And ponder it in my heart.

Margaret Herbert
England

On Being a Woman

It's hard to separate
Women's issues
From my own self surrender.
Hard to hear
One more preaching
About denying my ego
When all I ache for
Is to discover her
Somewhere within me
Still intact.

Diane D'Souza
south India/England

Silence

Too many women in too many countries
        speak the same language of silence.
My grandmother was always silent –
        always aggrieved –
Only her husband had the cosmic right
        (or so it was said) to speak and be heard.

They say it is different now
(after all, I am always vocal
        and my grandmother thinks I talk too much).
But sometimes, I wonder.

When a woman gives her love,
        as most women do, generously –
        it is accepted.

When a woman shares her thoughts,
        as some women do, graciously –
        it is allowed.

When a woman fights for power,
        as all women would like to,
        quietly or loudly,
        it is questioned.

And yet, there must be freedom –
        if we are to speak.
And yes, there must be power –
        if we are to be heard.
And when we have both (freedom and power),
        let us not be misunderstood.

We seek only to give words
       to those who cannot speak
       (too many women in too many countries).
I seek only to forget the sorrows
       of my grandmother's
       silence.

Anasuya Sengupta
south India

Taking Measure

I am struggling
With worth
Self worth.
Walls and boundaries
Dissolving
In abundant
Frightening
Freedom.
What is it you want?
What is this life?
Which direction to go?
Hearing the expectancy
In the silence
Listening for the echoes
Of steps not yet taken.

Diane D'Souza
south India/ England

Caged Bird

Like a caged bird
trapped inside the bars
of others' expectations of me,
singing a false, discordant tune;
I long
to spread my wings,
fly free,
let Him lift me
on the thermals of His love,
soar high up in the clouds in wondrous,
      free, expressive flight
and sing in harmony
once more.

Pat Marsh
England

Hey, This Is Me

Hey there, this is me ...
And I want to say
I'm not the me you seem to think I am.
The person whom you think you see
Is none but a reflection
Of the image you have built up in your head.
Maybe that's for you the easier way.
There isn't any risk in only looking at
The me you'd like to see.

But I want to say
Hey, this is me.

I'd really like to share with you
The bits that you are blind to,
Reveal to you the dreams
Which you simply fail to see,
Help you face
Whatever you're afraid that you won't like.
For the me that lies behind
That other me you choose to see
Longs to share with you the secrets of my heart,
To skip with you and dance with you
And celebrate the wonder
Of the way that we have changed as we have grown.

Hey, look there, this is me.
I can't be any other than the person that I am
And this is who I am
At this moment in my life.

Hey, this is me.

Just look a little deeper, if you can.

Pat Marsh
England

The Butterfly

Plodding.
Through mud
and grime
the dirt of other people's lives
and the way this world
is not as it should be.

Drugs
and debt
and crime
and abuse
and violence
and guns
and fear
and no escape
and 1 in 4 living
no, not living,
barely surviving
on just $1 a day.

And the church
worried more
about declining numbers
than about the way
the world
is not as it should be.

And I am dragged
down.
Plodding.
Through mud
and grime
through the dirt of my own life
and its inability
to change
the world
into that
which it was meant to be.

God
How do I change
this caterpillar existence?
How do I leave
the confines
of this plodding shell?
How do I break free?
How do I find the wings
to fly
to dazzle
to fill my life
with colour
and to transform
the world
into
a glorious butterfly?

Jenny Spouge
England

No-one Can Share My Inner Space

No one can share my inner space,
There I am alone, yet not alone:
For you are there, O God,
Deeper than my thinking,
Deeper than my feeling,
You are there, you are there O God,
Ever present mystery.

No one can share my inner space,
There I am alone, yet not alone:
For you are there, my friends,
Found within my thinking,
Dwelling in my dreaming,
You are there, you are there my friends,
Ever present mystery.

Discovering Ourselves

No one can share my inner space,
There I am alone, yet not alone:
For my family trees live on,
Live in tribal memory,
Live as genes great spiral,
You are here as trunk and branch
Ever present mystery.

No one can share my inner space,
There I am alone, yet not alone:
For we are part of Earth,
Sharing in one network,
Woven as one fabric,
We are strands of the web of life,
Ever present mystery.

W L Wallace
Aotearoa New Zealand

Lonely Out Here

It's lonely out here
with a chill wind blowing,
lonely out here,
and barely a snowdrop showing.

You want me to fit in a mould
that is not of my choosing;
the hollows are in the wrong place,
the air thick and confusing.

It's lonely out here
with a cold wind blowing,
lonely out here –
but I'll choose the way that I'm going.

Cecily Taylor
England

They

I'm afraid they might hurt you.
I'm afraid they might call you names.
I'm afraid they will blame me.
I'm afraid you will be persecuted,
Have fewer opportunities.
I'm afraid you will always have
To be secretive.
I'm afraid of what our family.
My friends, the neighbours will say.
I'm afraid to put the smiling pictures
Of you and your partners on the
Mantelpiece in the sitting room.
I'm afraid I need to explain.

I want to be unafraid
I want to say with joy
That both my children are gay.
I want to protect them from all
The ugliness of words,
The prejudice of they –
And I want to tell all the churchmen
God made you that way.

Elizabeth Cambridge
England

I'm Not Just A Back

I'm not just a back
I'm complete
I have a front, sides
A top
and a bottom.

I do the things you do
but slower
and with pain.
Take stock and look around
while waiting for me to catch up.

I have a voice
and my essence, my being
can run like the wind
I can go forwards as well as backwards.

Geoffrey Herbert
England

As for the Grass

When the lawn mower got nicked again,
I remembered that Jesus said:
'Don't worry about the grass
It's here today and gone tomorrow'.

So don't worry about the lawn mower.
You'll not add a hair to your head
Tomorrow has enough worries of its own,
As we worriers know only too well.

There's always the 'what ifs'
There's always the 'if onlys'
Mow them down
Weed them out.
Don't worry about the grass.
Sleep deep and dream of sheep.

Janet Lees
England

Blind Abseiling

The voice said 'come',
and though I could not see through the darkness,
I knew I must believe.
So I moved toward the voice,
gently feeling the way,
trusting in what he would tell me.

The voice said 'jump',
trust in me to hold you, you will not fall.
I knew I must believe,
So I jumped at his command,
letting myself go,
trusting in what he had told me.

The voice said 'love',
and held me until I was safe, guiding me to the light.
I do believe that in my heights
and depths and darkness,
all things can be done,
trusting in God's guidance.

Colin Ferguson
England

Dad, I Want My Stabilisers Back On

Dad, I want my stabilisers back on.
Didn't you see that wobble?
Didn't you feel my panic?
And hear my frightened cry?
Dad, I want my stabilisers back on.
The road's too rough,
The hill too steep.
The speed too much for me.
Dad –

My child
I saw your wobble
And heard your frightened cry.
I feel your panic
And know the road ahead.
But, as you reach for stabilisers
I see a greater gift
Of balance from within.
See latent skills
Swing into play.

New feelings already
Rising deep within
Dispelling fear
To leave you in control.
Unafraid to do my work
When you have none to help
But Me.
Fly child.
Fly like the wind.
Your safety rests with Me.

Hugh McKee
England

A Prayer for God's Blessing on a Homosexual Union

Blessed are you, O God.
Holy is your presence,
glorious is your peace.
You made humans to love and be loved.
You call us together into community
so that we might not live and die alone.
Bless now N1 and N2
as they commit themselves to one another.
As you have blessed your faithful people
throughout time and around the earth,
we ask you now to bless the union of their lives.

Blessed are you, O God, Father of mercies.
Pour your mercy over N2 and N1,
that they may know your loving kindness
and share your mercy with one another.

Blessed are you, O God, mother of life.
Create for N1 and N2 countless occasions
that they may share their life with the world.

Blessed are you, O God; you are our home.
Abide in their dwelling,
that it may be a place of warmth and protection,
hospitality and generosity.

Blessed are you, O God: you are the Horizon of our days.
Appear always before them,
that they may journey into their future
with you ever in their view.

Blessed are you, O God: you are the everlasting arms.
Protect them from danger,
support them in trouble,
comfort them in sorrow.
Embrace them with your tender strength
all the days of their lives.

Blessed are you, O God, Father, Son and Spirit.
the Lover, the Beloved, and Love.
Give to N2 and N1 and to all people
your love that passes understanding.
May we with the whole earth praise your goodness
now and forever.
Amen.

Gail Ramshaw
Canada

Two Sides to a Coin

In your insecurity,
    You judge us as being judgmental.

But like you,
    We simply seek the Word of God

And,
    In our insecurity,

Like to believe
    That we have found it.

Paul Friett
England

Roses At My Feet

Life's pathway
Stretches out before me,
Roses at my feet
Ablaze with brilliant colour.
God's own children
Alive from war and famine
And every kind of personal grief.
Each blooming now
In God's own presence,
Pressing close
To urge me on with news
Of what they found
Beyond the grave.
Light and Love,
Peace and Joy;
Dignity and self-worth,
As at Your feet
They left their burdens,
Sorrows, pain
And found instead
The Life you promised,
Far beyond their dreams.

So now they urge me on,
Lest I should stumble
In my darkness,
Thinking all is lost.
"Walk on" they call,
"Go through" they say,
He's there with you,
Arms wide with Love
And Resurrection Hope.

O Lord,
I hear them call.
I will press on this day
And in my darkness
Walk on with you,
Roses at my feet.

Hugh McKee
England

Charity?

We do not offer charity
But love, in human parity:
Acceptance of a fellow man
Just as we believe God can.

And does, not from a sympathy
But Love in divine empathy,
Justifying fallen man
Accepting as only God can.

Paul Friett
England

Moods

Life is grey
like the rain
falling on my window pane.
On the street
people stare,
no-one's going anywhere.
Empty days,
nights so long.
Can't help feeling
I'm all wrong.
Life is grey.

Comes the sun,
clears the sky.
Now my spirit's
soaring high.
Lots to do
and I must go,
why is everyone so slow?
Can't they see
life is good?
Surely everybody should –
In the sun?

Marjorie Dobson
England

Soft Wounds of Brush on Canvas
(An Artist's Hymn)

Soft wounds of brush on canvas,
the scraping of a knife,
the industry and artistry,
that gives a picture life;

And God carved in millennia,
through geologic time,
the pattern and the picture
divinity's design.

With hesitance we follow,
we mimic in our ways
amazing creativity
and, through this, offer praise.

7.6.7.6.
Andrew Pratt
England

Time Matrix
(for William)

I have been kept busy
Peeling back the layers
Of time,
And discovering that each
Isolated chord
In our own musical progression
Is inextricably
Interwoven with the others
In a complex,
Ongoing relationship
Of tension and resolution.

Examining the score
In greater detail,
We can each trace
Our own contribution
To the underlying
Harmonic texture,
And if my part
Should suddenly require
Several bars' rest
In the dynamic field
Of physical reality,
It is only for God's purpose
Of letting in
The light

Rosemary Parrott
England

O Christ, within Your Heart and Mind

O Christ, within your heart and mind
Three streams emerged and joined as one.
The man who spoke with prophet's fire
Showed mother-love and childlike fun.

The pattern you enshrined in flesh,
A trilogy of inner health,
We long to hold within our lives
A manly, childlike, female wealth.

But pow'r and wealth are still misused
Denying people's hope and pains;
You call us, Christ, to share our power
And break all life-denying chains.

You free us all to laugh and cry,
To love and touch released from fear;
To nurture earth and all her kind
Through God, the source of all true care.

God help us all, with childlike joy,
Affirm our strength and tenderness,
That male and female in our hearts
May be as one in graciousness.

W L Wallace
Aotearoa New Zealand

Fingerprints

Gently working,
Potter's hands;
Kneading, shaping,
Softening clay.
Moulding, flexing,
Changing form,
With skilful eyes the guide
To see
Beyond the lump of lifeless clay
A vision of what lies within:
Potential yet to come to birth,
Created from his loving touch
And his fingertip imprints
On the clay.

Lord, let me be
As clay within Your hands,
That You may shape
The me You hold within Your dreams
And I may know
Your fingerprints
Upon my life.

Pat Marsh
England

Accompanied All the Way
(A Reflection on Psalm 139)

Bless you Wise and Holy One
        for your universal presence –
If I sink into the deepest ocean
        you are there
If I soar beyond Orion
        you are there
If I take the wings of the morning
ascend to high noon
and plunge to the depths of midnight
        you are there
Where could I outsoar your Spirit?
Where could I outdistance your presence?

Bless you Wise and holy One
        for your indismissable presence –
When my equations factor you out
When my intellect scoffs

Discovering Ourselves

When my reason turns its back
    you are still there
How could I dismiss your spirit?
How could I explain away your presence?

Such presence is too awesome for me
    too large for my equations
    too deep for my explanations
I cannot contain it
I simply acknowledge –
    it contains me
Bless you
    Uncontainable
    Indismissable
    Universal One

Norm S D Esdon
Canada

Discoveries

Leaves are whispering to ageing summer
enticing me along the path to the damp wood.
The path guides me to the brook,
and the brook shows me
where it meets its companion,
which in turn leads me to the waterfall.

The waterfall sings of the bevy of wild cyclamen
in silken bloom along its bank,
and nine surprised toadstools
see a scurrying water-rat
in a hurry to reach home –
much too busy to share a secret.

But I have found a fledgling's empty shell
and this tells of the new me which has just hatched!

Cecily Taylor
England

Becoming A More Responsible People

They Will Come ...

From East and West they will come,
from North and South
the faithful and the doubter
the speaker and the listener
the first-timer and the experienced
the confident and the apprehensive
bound together by their faith in Jesus Christ
gathering to remember the story of God amongst us
letting the Holy Spirit stir up deep hope within us.
God's people will gather – let us worship God!

The United Reformed Church

A Wife Farms the Land

Jettaiah and his wife Bathamma have six children: two boys and four girls. They live in a village in Andra Pradesh State, south India Three of the girls are married and live with their in-laws.

Jettaiah has a physical disability which affects his mobility. Despite this impairment he is able to earn some money for the family by watching over the buffaloes of other people. Meanwhile his wife, Bathamma farms their land. The family does not have their own bullocks so they make an arrangement with someone else to plough their land in return for a 25% share of the eventual crop.

Bathamma has collected manure and is applying this to her one and half acres of wasteland in order to increase its productivity. This wasteland was given by the government but without support for developing the land. The Find Your Feet project has enabled Bathamma to pay a small amount for the labour to help upgrade the land. This has been done by removing many of the stones from the land and digging bunds around the land which serve the purpose of harvesting rain water and preventing the run-off of rain which causes heavy soil erosion.

This is the first time that Bathamma has been able to use the wasteland. She is planning to grow sorgham , red gram, * green gram, * green vegetables, and field beans. The seeds will come from the crops she has grown on her other half acre of land.

* seed

Find Your Feet
England /south India

Saying NO
(Reading; Exodus 1:8–2:10)

Work them to death!
Kill their babies!
Hate, despise, destroy, dehumanise
The immigrant workers, underclass

In every oppressive system
there are people who say NO.
The midwives used to saving life,
would not deal in death.
Moses lived
because of the subversive courage
of women: bringer of God's Law,
born in an unjust state.

God of justice, help us to stand firm
against the unjust practices
of our time;
give us the courage to say NO
when human rights are disregarded,
prejudices reinforced, people
stereotyped,
dehumanised, enslaved.
Show us how
to subvert when we cannot confront
the baby-killers of our time.

Heather Pencavel
England.

She Is A Broken Child

This is a story of a special child,
from the barren land of north Karnataka *
where people live each moment at the mercy of God,
their eyes affixed upward waiting,
for the rain to quench the thirst of the land,
morsel of food is a real gift.

This is a reality of a lonely child, dressed in rags,.
lost her mother while she was still a baby,
battered by her third step-mother,
punished each day for her limitation to
earn bread for the family.

She was raped by her own grand old man,
fighting between life and death,
conceived a baby, lost it soon after.
She cries in silence, cries all alone,
unaware of the harshness of the world.

This is the truth of a little child,
her voice lost in the wilderness,
Who dares to listen to this cry?
Who is there to reach out to her
on that barren land?

Someday when her pangs of hunger are painful
she flees to the hills,
speaking to the trees for comfort
fills her stomach with wild berries and leaves.
She is a broken child,
She is a lonely child.

She suffers with pain from bruises
for no fault of hers
her heart bleeds for love, yet she survives
each day with an indomitable will.
She is a broken child.
She is a special child.
* Karnataka is a state in south India

M R Manohar
south India

Lives Have Been Broken

Lives have been broken. Peace has been shattered.
Words have been spoken best left unsaid.
Lying around us, remnants of loving.
Joy out of focus, happiness dead.

Careless of feeling, trampling onwards –
barely concealing lack of concern –
hurting and bleeding follow our actions,
Where is it leading? When will we learn?

Stark and revealing, comes that dark moment,
when broken feeling makes us aware.
All we have shattered, all we have broken,
loving that mattered, no longer there.

Then comes the sorrow. Realisation!
What of tomorrow? Torment, remorse!
Lord, grant us healing in our awareness,
your love revealing compassion's source.

Lord take our sadness. Grant us renewal.
Out of this madness help us to see,
as we rebuild life and beg forgiveness
we find your new life setting us free.

Marjorie Dobson
England

I Have Called You by Your Name and You Are Mine
(In memory of people who have died street-homeless)

God says, 'I have called you by your name and you are mine.'

God of love, call me by my name. Pronounce its syllable with care. Speak my full name, the name the world knows me by. Speak my private names, known only to my friends. My lovers, myself.

You know me from my beginning to my end. Speak my name and make me yours, for ever.

God says, 'Your name is engraved on the palm of my hand.'

God of infinite tenderness who hurt your hand with my name? How did my name get cut into your palm? How did the blade wound your skin?

But when you curl your hand, my name is there, held in your powerful, gentle hand. Keep me safe, hold me tight, and let me never hurt you, or anyone again.

God says, 'I will give you a new name, known only to the one who receives it.'

God of power, you have the right to name me. You have known my character as it developed. You have seen my good times and been with me in my bad times. You know when I have spat and cursed and damaged those around me. You know when I have charmed and loved and helped to heal.

Let me come close to you, so that I can hear my name. You know the one that only you and I, only you and I, will ever know.

God says, 'I have called you by your name and you are mine.'

God of love, you speak the name of every person on earth. When we lean towards you, you speak our names and make us yours. When we turn to the world, we know the amazing truth that this same intimate love, this same total dignity, belongs to all the people we meet.

Give us the loving strength to honour every name and every person. Speak to us the names of the people we meet, remind us that you have called them by their names and all belong to you.

Janet Wootton
England

Cry from the Desert Sand

Far away in the wilderness
I hear the
desert winds sweeping
with fury
the roar so chill, with
it the cries of agony and death.

Far away in the deep sands,
I hear the human voices
hidden below, their breath has smell of fear
waiting for death
to take them up from their
bunkers.

Oh God
save this humankind
from destruction and war
save these children
who are victims
of human folly
from perishing.

M R Manohar
south India

Pray for Those Who Suffer

Lord Jesus Christ, Prince of Peace, you tell us to pray for peace and to love
our enemies. We pray for those, both governments and manufacturers,
involved in making and selling weapons and for those who use weapons,
sometimes against their own wishes. We also pray for those who suffer as
a result of those weapons; those injured by landmines, bereaved by bombs
and bullets or traumatised by the horrors of war. We pray for those children
pushed into fighting often for causes they do not understand and for those
who use them as foot-soldiers.
Amen

Danielle and Naomi Bowdler
England

Those Who Are Left Behind

Sleepless, eyes hot with tears,
I face another dawn,
With only memories to keep me warm,
They tell me that the pain will ease,
Perhaps its true, till then,
Each day I taste the heartbreak once again,
For war has taken one I love,
And desolate and lonely, I am left behind.

When the darkness of war is over
And we move into the light,
There are so many for whom, the fight,
Has only just begun,
Widows and orphans, parents who grieve
For a daughter or a son,
Casualties who did not die,
But are maimed, in body or in mind,
The all too many victims that war has left behind.

And you that make decisions,
For the future of mankind,
Think when you count up the casualties,
Not only of the fallen,
But of those they leave behind.

Doreen Gazey
England

A Prayer of Confession

We confess complicity and indifference ...
We do not allow the suffering of others to disturb our comfort
We forget our countries' history and deny responsibility.

Kyrie, kyrie, eleison. Kyrie, kyrie, eleison.

We confess our ignorance ...
We have shut out the voices of those whose experiences are different from ours
We rely too much on the media to tell us what to think
We know only our own reality.

Kyrie, kyrie, eleison. Kyrie, kyrie, eleison.

We confess our evasion of silence ...
We allow our fear to control us
We have allowed evil to go unchecked
We try to confront the world's evils without ever confronting our own heart.

Kyrie, kyrie, eleison. Kyrie, kyrie, eleison.

Forgive us, O Lord, and help us to follow the path of peace in ourselves and for our world.

Claudia Genung Yamamoto
Christian Conference of Asia

I Could No Longer Support My Family

Muracin Claircin sold his plot of land, left his wife and two children and paid US$1,000 for a place on a boat to take him to the United States. 'I had to do this because I could no longer support my family by growing rice,' he explains.

After a tortuous week drifting at sea without enough food or water, the captain told them they would have to turn back because the ship's compass was broken. Now back with his family, Muracin has neither money nor land and says that, given the opportunity, he would try again. He still cannot make a living from rice farming.

'There's no incentive to grow rice anymore. It's virtually impossible to make a profit,' said Miracin.

He is just one of the thousands of rice farmers in Haiti who have lost their livelihoods in the flood of cheap American imported rice. Fifteen years ago, Haiti was all but self-sufficient in rice, producing 180.000 tonnes. Today it produces 1000,000 tonnes – but imports of US rice have risen by over a half to 215,000 tonnes. Haiti's small farmers already impoverished and desperately trying to farm on small plots of land, have been unable to withstand the harshness and speed of economic liberalisation.

Christian Aid

A Time of Drought

Extreme weather. The earth become dust. The farm animals slaughtered and the water tanks empty. And the sun burning every leaf to powdery dust.

We pray for rain.
We pray for survival.
And we pray for solidarity.
God eternal, this drought may be
only the blink of an eye
on the timechart of history,
but for us it is an age,
days, weeks, months with no sign of rain,
and life slowly draining away in the dust.

May the whole community stand together,
sharing what we have.
May we be steadfast and never in despair.

And may the world learn – and learn – quickly –
that human life can make matters worse,
more drought, more floods, more barren soils,
because we are greedy and claim too much.

Help us now to love your creation
Bless us with rain
as you rain on us blessings
all our lives.

Bernard Thorogood
Australia

A Lifeline

Zahra lives in Afghanistan. She is sixteen and about to have her first child. Preventable infections and dangerous birthing practices used to kill up to six mothers a year and more than one baby each month. They used to have their own way of delivering babies and many died from common infections as did their mothers. The mother's shoes or a saw were used to cut the umbilical cord. The cord was not washed or tied. Dirty cotton wool from mattresses was placed on it. These practices have been averted now by the training of traditional birth attendants. Women got together and went to the Rural Rehabilitation Association of Afghanistan which is a partner of Christian Aid and asked to be trained. The attendants visit villages now taking a simple birthing kit which contains a bar of soap, a razor blade and an ordinary piece of string.

Christian Aid (adapted)

A Prayer of Dedication

Leader: In humility, let us commit ourselves to the pursuit of God's promise of life abundant, life with dignity and worth, life with justice and peace for our sisters and brothers and for all who amidst their pain and suffering continue to hope.

All: Lord Jesus we offer ourselves to always seek peace and affirm justice for all people; choosing struggle rather than indifference; choosing to be servants rather than masters; choosing to be peace makers rather than peace keepers; choosing life for all people rather than death.
May God help us.
Amen

Church of North India

The Motorist's Prayer

Grant me a ready hand, a watchful eye,
       That none may suffer hurt as I pass by.
Thou givest life – I pray no act of mine
       May take away or mar that gift of thine.
Should those, dear Lord, who bear my company,
       From fools and fire and all calamity.
Teach me to use my car for others' need,
       Nor miss through lack of wit or love of speed,
The beauty of Thy world – that this I may,
       With joy and courtesy go on my way.

Geraldine Binnall
England

Vulnerable God, Hear the Cries of Your People

Vulnerable God, hear the cries of your people,
cries that are wrung from our hearts filled with pain.
God in your justice give vent to compassion,
healing our hurt and uplifting again.

God of the cross, you have known crucifixion,
holding your course in the face of disdain,
Now as we suffer, we seek your conviction,
for shoots of life lurk in frost-hardened grain.

Vulnerable God, hear the cries of your people,
those we would slaughter as bombs fall like rain.
Help us to see through our raging and anger,
parents and children whose tears seem in vain.

Great God of love, while such anger consumes us,
grant the perspective that helps us stay sane;
then as we answer the foes who confound us,
through our response may our love be their gain.

Tune: Star in the East
Andrew Pratt
England

Look at People All Around

Written after a visit to a playground In Leyton, east London where visits are made by people from Pakistan, Turkey, South America, Eastern Europe and England. Later that day it was learned that United Nations personnel were being moved out of Iraq and that war was anticipated.

We look at people all around,
our friends from many nations;
some hardly known to us at all.
some known for generations.

The love of God, the bond that binds
us close to one another,
will help us face whatever comes
as sister and as brother.

We do not know what lies ahead
through war or devastation,
we only know what holds our lives
spans ours and every nation.

Your spirit that has brought us near
will help us face derision
as meeting with 'the enemy'
to love is our decision.

That love is stronger than the fear
That sows the seeds of hatred;
a love that we will keep alive
when all else has abated.

Andrew Pratt
England

Prayer for the Peace of Humankind

O God, in this world you create,
We see violence and wars every day.
We see assault, plunder, abuse, expulsion,
        killing and human trade.
We see conflicts among tribes.
We see terror, retaliation and wars among nations.
We see many people being killed and
        expelled from their land.
We see many people wandering to find a place to live.
We see desolated nature and
        the impoverished living environment.

O God,
We confess the violence is in us.
We attack, exclude, blame and hurt our neighbours
With our language, social position, political power,
        and relationships.

We oppress women, neglect children, ignore the poor,
And abuse foreign workers.
We pollute and damage nature thoughtlessly.

O God,
Please forgive us!
Please be within us and let your peace fill this world!
Please be with us and give us a thirst for peace!
Please let the river of peace flow within us!
Please stop wars and conflicts!
Please make us peacemakers!
Please strengthen and encourage us to stand against
All kinds of violence and wars!
We pray in the name of Jesus Christ, our Lord.
Amen

National Christian Council in Korea

A Prayer of Commitment to Non-violence

Leader: Loving God, you have entrusted us with the care of the earth, and called us to love one another

Response: Forgive us all that denies your trust.

Leader: Forgive us our willingness to develop the means of destruction at the expense of the things that create community.

Response: Forgive us all that denies your trust.

Leader: Forgive us that, when we are asked for bread, we offer defence contracts and deals, binding so many lives to the arms trade.

Response: Forgive us all that denies your trust.

Leader: By your forgiveness, free us to give ourselves fully to the eradication of the arms trade. Give us the courage to commit ourselves to peace with justice for all on this earth.

Response: God, teach us to trust you and live by love.

Leader: By your grace you have given us all that we need. Enable us to give up those things that we do not need – the idols of power, selfishness and greed.

Response: God, teach us to trust you and live by your love.

Leader: God, be with us in our work against the arms trade; be with us as we search for authentic ways of expressing our love for the world.

Response: God, teach us to trust you and live by your love.

Campaign Against Arms Trade
England

Sisters and Brothers in Chains

Father of humankind,
We remember before you:
People held in a poverty trap from which there is no escape;
Governments struggling on a treadmill of debt;
Landless peasants who are slaves to moneylenders;
Girls sold into prostitution because their parents have no other source of income;
Women whose opportunities and status are permanently restricted by the
traditions of religion and culture;
Indigenous people who are persecuted and driven from their tribal lands;
Street children in various countries who are rejected, unwanted and murdered;
Helpless ordinary people suffering under oppressive dictators or warlords;

And we remember the dictators, the oppressors, the slaves-to-money and the
slaves-to-power.

May the infection of a new compassion spread over each one, inspiring,
releasing, restoring and transforming.

Alan Litherland
England

Think It Over

Today:

 We have high yielding crops and more production than requirement.

Still, people are living in poverty
        with hunger and starvation in developing countries.

We have short–term goals
        but shorter tempers
We preach more
        but practice less
We have bigger ambitions
        but narrower points of view
We have more knowledge
        but less judgement
We have more professions and advanced medicine
        but less health.
We have multiplied our possessions
        but reduced our values.
We have reached the moon and come back
        but we find it troublesome to cross our own street
        to meet our neighbours

We have conquered outer space
    but not found our inner space.
We have high incomes
    but less morality
We have more liberty
    but less joy and happiness

These are the days in which it takes two salaries for each home
    but less time to spend with our own children.

We talk too much
    we love only a little
      we hate too much.

So, as of today:

Don't keep anything for a special occasion
    because everyday of life is a special occasion.
Search for knowledge, read more,
    sit on your relaxing chair and admire the view
    without paying attention to your needs.
Spend more time with your family, relatives and friends,
    and visit the places you love to see.
Life should be a chain of joyful moments,
    and not only about existence.
Use your crystal goblets.
Do not save your best perfume but use it every time you feel you want to.
Let's tell all our families, relatives and friends how much we love them.
Do anything that adds laughter and joy to your life.
Every day, every hour, every minute and every second is special.
And you don't know if it will be your last.

Anil Kumar Patil
south India/England

Pestalozzi
(Education Today for Tomorrow's World)

The following is an extract from a letter sent to a supporter by the Director of Pestalozzi International Village Trust

''Some years ago, His Holiness The 14th Dalai Lama said:

'Whether we like it or not, we have all been on this earth as part of one great human family. Rich or poor, educated or uneducated, belonging to one nation or another, to one religion or another, adhering to this ideology or that, ultimately each of us is just a human being like everyone else: we all desire happiness and do not want suffering. Further, each of us has an equal right to pursue these goals.

'Today's world requires that we accept the oneness of humanity. In the past, isolated communities could afford to think of another as fundamentally separate and even existed in total isolation. Nowadays, however, events in one part of the world eventually affect the entire planet. Therefore we have to treat each major local problem as a global concern from the moment it begins. We can no longer invoke the national, racial or ideological barriers that separate us without destructive repercussion. In the context of our new interdependence, considering the interests of others is clearly the best form of self-interest.

'I view this fact as a source of hope.''

Original Source Unknown
Pestalozzi International Village Trust
England

They Heal Their Bodies ...
They Heal the Earth

She bleeds
With every slash on her body
She weeps!
The electric saw cuts deep ... cuts quickly
Into the gentle flesh of the trees.
The trees weep!
And slowly forests die ...
The soil dies ...
The earth dies
And God knows that the earth weeps
And weeps with her.

She bleeds,
With every battering of her body
She weeps!
His hand has power ... it cuts deeply
Into the gentle flesh of her soul.
We all weep
Slowly the women die ...
The community dies ...
The earth dies
And God knows that the women weep
And weeps with them.

The women resist the saw.
The audacious might of the profit seeking contractor.
The women use their wounded bodies
To save their trees.
The only form of resistance open to them,
They cling to the trees defying death.
They stop the saw.

They stop the flow of blood.
They heal the forests,
They heal the earth.

The women resist the violence
The arrogant might of the 'brave and strong' one.
The women transcend their suffering and pain
To save their lives.
The only form of strength they have.
They come together in a circle of power
They cling to each other's tears.
They stop the hurt and pain.
They heal the community.
They heal the earth.

Women of the Chipko movement,
Women of the earth,
Women of life ...
Women of survivors of violence,
Women of hope ...
They weep no more,
They heal their bodies,
They heal the earth ...
And God laughs with uninhibited joy!

Aruna Gnanadason
India/Switzerland

The Psychological Trauma of War on Children
(Medical Aid for Iraqi Children)

The tragedy that has befallen the Iraqi children over the past thirteen years will go down in history as one of the worst of its kind.

Children make up the most vulnerable sector of the Iraqi society. They have paid dearly as a result of the damaging effects of two wars on Iraq in 1991 and 2003 and the implementation of a damaging United Nations (UN) sanctions on the country between 1990 and 2003.

As Chairman of Medical Aid for Iraqi children (MAIC), a British Registered Charity founded in 1995, I have witnessed through my several visits to children's hospitals in Iraq, the suffering and tragic health conditions of this young population.

My realisation of the severity of the fall of living standards began the first night I arrived in Baghdad in 1995. Whilst I was preparing for my visit the next day to the paediatric hospitals, I put aside a bag filled with little snacks bought in London to distribute to the sick children at the hospitals. When my 21 year-old nephew learned of my intention he looked at me with astonishment and said, 'Do you know how much each of those snacks is worth? And that's assuming it can found on the black market' he continued to say that each tube of sweets was worth 3500 dinars, equivalent to one month's salary for an average hospital employee. This was my first shocking encounter with the collapse of the country's economy.

Visiting Iraqi hospitals between 1995 and 2000 has been painful and shocking experience. I have seen broken windows, soiled mattresses, while sheets and blankets did not exist. Sanitary facilities were out of order due to the breakdown of the sewage system and lack of spare parts. Items for repair such as new pipes and water purification agents have been blocked by UN sanctions committee as dual use items. Children suffering because of the lack of medication. Parents gaze at you and beg you to help their loved ones.

The collapse of the Iraqi health system since 1990 and its repercussions on children are described in the first published reports by the UN in 1991. Iraq in the mid 1980s was described as a state that had an elaborate health care system. Mortality rates between both infants and children under five declined between 1984 and 1989. However, the trend rapidly reversed in the 1990s. In 1998 the UN estimated that there was a total of 570,000 children dead because of sanctions. Since then, adding up the extra deaths on the basis of the 1990s trend there would be over one million children dead to date. Moreover, according to a more recent UNICEF report published in 2003, the mortality rate of children under five was 133 per 1000 live births in 2001 compared to 50 in 1990. According to a UNICEF report of 18 February 2003, 'one out of eight Iraqi children die before the age of five, one of the worst rates in the world'.

One of the most damaging effect of the 1991 Gulf War was the bombing of the Iraqi infrastructure mainly electricity and the sewage system. The breakdown of the sewage system and the resulting contamination of the main water supplies resulted in breeding a large spectrum of water borne diseases and infections. Another grave consequence of the shelling is the pollution and contamination in the country causing a major health hazard. Since the 1991 war cancer and in particular leukaemia among children has increased up to four fold in some areas. We have also witnessed a sharp increase in birth deformities and miscarriages. Moreover, the implementation of UN sanctions drastically slowed down the capability of repairing the electricity and water supplies. It also greatly reduced the supply of food and medicines due to the long and bureaucratic process of applying to the UN Sanctions Committee for approving export of essential needs. All these factors resulted in catastrophic humanitarian tragedy. Rise in mortality rates among infants, severe malnutrition especially between children and women and general protein and mineral deficiencies among the population at large. It also resulted in severe shortages of medical supplies which caused unnecessary deaths of children from simple ailments, where they could have been easily treated.

The 2003 war and its aftermath added further devastation to an already shattered economy and hardship to the Iraqi people. Scores of civilians and especially children died and many more were injured and maimed. Until now there is no official count of the dead and injured among the Iraqi people.

Although the occupying forces have kept a record of the dead and injured among their troops they did not keep a parallel record for the Iraqi troops and civilians. However, independent estimates put the figure at around 10,000 civilian deaths to date.

The countryside is still littered with unexploded ordnance (UXO) from the past wars such as bomblets from cluster bombs. There is also the damage resulting from unattended ammunition dumps which have caused death and maiming to many Iraqis. According to UNICEF more than 1000 children have died since the end of the 2003 war as a result of the explosions at ammunition depots and from cluster bombs.

The use of depleted uranium by the coalition in 2003 was at least three fold of what was used in 1991. This has led to an increase of respiratory problems and digestive system ailments. The overall effects in health are still to early to predict. However, increase in cancers, weaknesses in the immune systems and birth deformities are major issues to be monitored.

Furthermore, the psychological trauma of the wars on children will have long term disturbing effects. According to UNICEF before the 2003 war an estimated 500,000 children will be in need of psychiatric help.

These are urgent issues that need to be addressed. The international community did little in the past to give the Iraqi children the protection and care they are entitled to as part of the children of the world. They have not been represented in children's forums and were not sufficiently mentioned in the agenda of many international organisations dealing with the wellbeing of children. It is urgent that the international community come together and invest in a constructive programme to help the children in Iraq.

Medical Aid for Iraqi Children (MAIC) is one of a handful of charities working in Iraq since 1995. Over the past eight years we have been supplying paediatric hospitals with medicines and medical equipment totalling, in value, over £2 million. MAIC's real strength lies in its targeted aid which supplies hospitals with their specific medical requirements. We estimate that we were able to treat over 180,000 children with our modest funds.

Following the 2003 war, MAIC had to expand its medical aid to provide paediatric hospitals with their growing list of requirements. Not only are we supplying hospitals with their regular lists of medicines but also with other medical supplies such as surgical items, wheelchairs and crutches and medicines to treat patients suffering from infections, burns and injuries which have increased since the onset of war and in its aftermath. We have also been supplying hospitals with medical equipment to replace the ones looted and destroyed such as incubators.

At present the process of change in running the vital amenities is still slow and inefficient. The oil for food programme will be running out shortly and there is no clear foresight for a replacement plan. There is also no clear budget for the health sector. Therefore, the challenges facing humanitarian agencies to increase aid during this crucial period are even greater.

May Al-Daftari
Iraq/England

Help the Children ...

Dear God,
Help the children of Iraq* through the night. I will sleep safely and soundly but they will be woken by sirens and explosions. Keep them safe.

* Iraq may be replaced by the names of other countries according to the time this prayer is used.

Hywel Nevard (age 10)
England

Are You My Neighbour?

I am standing in front of you.
Even though I am an orphan
Life must continue
I have no mother, no father,
Life is difficult.

When I am hungry, I miss my parents
When I am sick I miss my parents
I have no mother, no father
Life is difficult.

My friends go to school
To learn to read and write
I remain at home
I feel I am not important

What will you do?
What shall I do?
I'm requesting to live, just to live
I have no mother, no father
Life is so difficult.

An anonymous ten year old boy
Badelika Project
Kenya

A Litany for the World's Children
This Litany is commended for All Age Worship

Leader   Let the children come to me and do not stop them
                the kingdom of God belongs to such as these.

Children   Lord Jesus your kingdom belongs to us.

Child 1   I love fruit pastilles
                I'll share them with you
                I can buy more tomorrow
                and still have pocket money left.

Child 2
In my country
one of those tubes
would cost my father
a whole month's wages.

Leader
Let the children come to me and do not stop them
the kingdom of God belongs to such as these.

Children
Lord Jesus your kingdom belongs to us.

Child 3
It's time for bed
I've been to the toilet and cleaned my teeth
Mum turns out the light and I snuggle down
under my warm duvet

Child 4
I don't know the time
it's dark and we have no light
I'll need to use the bucket outside
Then lie on my mattress and try to sleep.

Leader
Let the children come to me and do not stop them
the kingdom of God belongs to such as these.

Children
Lord Jesus, your kingdom belongs to us.

Child 5
I need an operation on my ear
so that I will be able to hear better
I'm a bit scared of hospital, but
they've got a computer you can play on.

Child 6
My baby brother is very sick
but the hospital has no medicine
if he doesn't get treatment soon
he will die.

Leader
Let the children come to me and do not stop them
the kingdom of God belongs to such as these.

Children
Lord Jesus, your kingdom belongs to us.

Child 7
I went for a walk today with my friends
we went to the woods
and had brilliant fun
playing hide and seek.

Child 8
We have to be so careful
where we walk

> my friend lost a leg last week
> when an unexploded mine went off.

Leader   Let the children come to me and do not stop them
the kingdom of God belongs to such as these.

Children   Lord Jesus, your kingdom belongs to us
and we belong to you
Hear our prayers
Let the world hear our cries
Let your kingdom come on earth
For us
NOW.

Heather Johnston
England

A Litany for the Children of War

Where systems collapse into chaos and confusion
And dirt and despair spread like a cancer
We hear the cries of the Christ-child
In the pain of the children of war.

Where the price of a tube of sweets is a month's wages
And children die for lack of food and medicine
We hear the cries of the Christ-child
In the pain of the children of war.

Where parents with pleading eyes watch little ones suffer
Whilst doctors and nurses try to heal with empty hands
We hear the cries of the Christ-child
In the pain of the children of war.

Where bombs continue to hurt, maim and destroy
Long after the raids have ended
We hear the cries of the Christ-child
In the pain of the children of war.

Where injuries fester and memories torment
And trauma leaves its scars for years to come
We hear the cries of the Christ-child
In the pain of the children of war.

In the struggle to bring help and healing
In the dream of peace after violence
God, born anew in the Christ-child
Bring hope to the children of war.

Jan Berry
England

Scene Changes

God the Weaver

God the weaver, making patterns,
Spinning threads throughout our days –
Joy and sadness interwoven,
Strands of sorrow, strands of praise.
Help us to discern your weaving
In the multi-coloured maze.

Teach us, Lord, to trust your guidance
When the pattern is not clear,
And to feel your strength and comfort
When life's fabric's torn by fear.
Help us sense that in the dark times
Lightening love is always near.

When we see the pattern changing
And a new direction starts,
Let us know your love unbroken
Winds through life is all its parts
By the threads of love and friendship
Closely woven in our hearts.

Though we never see the picture
With your sense of space and time,
Help us, Lord, to take our places
In our faith's continuing line,
As all lives are interwoven
In your final grand design.

Tune: 8.7.8.7.8.7.
Marjorie Dobson
England

What Will You Do?

What will you do
when the children have grown
flown away?
Will you rest in the shade
made empty?
Or will you launch a boat
float on impossible waterways?

Scene Changes

Excuse me if I do not stay
talking here to you –
but I have secret timbers to hew
and a keel to lay.

Cecily Taylor
England

Departure Lounge
(Prelude to a Gap Year)

Heathrow
Terminal Four.

Nice day for a journey.

Can my mind really squeeze a lifetime,
Your lifetime,
Into this last precious hour.

It seems it can.

No looking back from you
As you head off towards the check-in desk.
Watching you, striding out,
My mind replay
The way that those same legs
Kicked footballs on a muddy field, week in, week out.

Clothed now in brand new expedition trews
(Crease-proof, lightweight, the special gear),
but in your younger days
more likely to be crawling, belly down,
in tattered camouflage greens:
the solider hero,
eight, going on twenty-eight,
who battled with his brother in the undergrowth.

I watch you
Organising visas, passports, tickets,
Paperwork which gives consent for you
To fly so far away from me.
I look at the confidence within you
And think of the six year old with stage fright;
The little shepherd
With the tee towel round his head.

I'll send you a photograph, you say,
From the top of the tallest building
In the world.
Kuala Lumpur, I think it is,
But in my mind
I'm back at the top of a castle wall,
With a little seven year old, so terrified of such a tiny height.

Posing for a final picture with your girl,
I feel a pang of jealousy,
A sense of loss,
At knowing she's the one that you'll confide in now,
And that my work of motherhood
Is done.
Seeing your strong arm around her waist
I remember the night you hugged and held me through
When Granddad died.
I'll miss him so, you said.
And the memory of that moment
Triggers tears in me
As I want to echo now those very words to you.

And I watch you
As you walk away.

My eyes don't want to leave you
As you go.
They linger on your image
As if a powerful magnet holds them there.

Down the corridor
To Departure Lounge, Terminal Four
And beyond that
To The World.

I look.
Yes, I look
At my little boy

As he walks away

And now

I see the man.

Nice day.
Nice day for a journey.

Pat Marsh
England

Persistent God

Persistent God
you are no respector of old age
        and you never have been.
You called so many people
long after others had assumed their useful lives were over.

Abraham was asked to move to a new country
        and take on a new name.
Sarah had her child long after it was thought possible.
Moses grew tetchy and weary leading rebellious people
        on a wilderness journey.
Elizabeth was far too old to be the mother of John the Baptist,
        but that didn't stop you from choosing her.
And how rapidly Mary must have aged
        as she realised what was happening to her son, Jesus.

Never-ageing God,
When growing old in your service
        seems to be a very tiring process,
Help us to remember the challenges you gave
        to these older people.

Teach us that we are never too old for new experiences.
Forgive us when we use our world-weariness
        to dampen the enthusiasm of youth.
Remind us that though we may be lacking in energy,
        they are not.
Keep us young in heart and spirit, even if our bodies protest,
        for your world is a place of active love
and all of us can be involved in that,
whatever our age.

Marjorie Dobson
England

God-Controlled

Controlled by God and not by tradition,
Loyal to Christ and not the institution.

For thine is the kingdom, Lord.

Called to service and not to slavery,
Following the Christ and not the crowds.

For thine is the power, Lord.

Conforming to God's will and not the world's,
Living to please God and not pleasing myself.

For thine is the glory, Lord.

Counting all things loss for the sake of Christ,
Obeying the Word of God and not the words of religion.

For ever and ever, Lord.

Frances Ballantyne
England

Threshold

Lord, how I've longed for, anticipated,
Prayed for this moment,
Dreamt it in my heart,
Even, oftimes, stirred from my slumbers
Thinking of it.
And yet, Lord,
It doesn't feel easy,
Standing on the threshold
Of this new beginning.

Wavering on the threshold of this new start, Lord,
I think I want to thank You.
I stand in awe
Of the marvellous way You answer prayer
Although it's rarely how I would have thought,
And never the way
I quietly suggested You might answer it.

Forgive my impatience in the past, Lord.
Now that I've arrived here
With clarity of insight
I see that You were always close
Through all those long uncertain times
When I was waiting:
Waiting for the quiet, unhurried
Unfolding of Your will.

Standing, poised,
On tiptoe as it were,
On the verge of this beginning;
The as yet untrodden future
Lying virgin, beckoning before;
I sense a moment pregnant with potential,
Brimful of opportunity
And hope;
Another point where past and future meet
And I may choose
Exactly which uncharted path to tread.

And yet I'm nervous, Lord.
The nervousness
Is in the starting out.
My eyes keep glancing backward
To the comfort zone of my familiar past.
I am somehow reluctant to begin, for fear I get it wrong,
Fail to fulfil the promise within me.

But, thank you, Lord
That you have brought me here,
Albeit by a route I never would have chosen for myself.

Just one more prayer Lord, if I may;
Stay close and lead me on.

My child
I understand your nervousness,
Can see how hard it is
For you to see where I am leading you
When you can't view the details of the path
From My divine perspective.

Give all your fears to Me.
Humble yourself beneath My mighty power.
Keep in mind
That all that lies ahead
Is cradled in My love,
Held gently in My nail scarred hands.
I will renew, support and strengthen you.
I will equip you, friend,
To help you live your dreams.

So come now, praise and celebrate
With every fibre of your soul
And from the threshold of this new beginning
Journey on with Me.
Step out in faith.
Step out
With Me.

Pat Marsh
England

A Litany of Freedom
(based on a poem by Rabindranath Tagore)

Leader: Where the people walk without fear, heads held high; where knowledge is free for all; where society has not been broken into fragments by narrow domestic walls; where the words of teachers and politicians spring from the depths of truth. Where the tireless striving of social reformers stretches its arms towards a new humanity; where the clear streams of creative culture has not lost its way in the desert sand of dead habits; where minds of leaders, scientists and writers are led forward by you in ever-widening thought and action.

Response: Into that freedom we long for, my Father, let my country awake.
Amen

Church of North India

Pray for a Big Change
(Written for a Lent Fast Day)

I turn towards the light
Like a plant on the sill
Stretching to glimpse the truth of hope

I raise my head to the sun
Like the crops in the earth
Reaching for the warmth of your mercy

I sway and seek the freshening rain
Unsure of my direction
Remembering the waters of my baptism

Like the mustard tree
My branches stretch to shelter
Searching for the ways to do your work

Compassionate God you know me
Hold me and direct me
Help me to water the seeds of your kingdom

Linda Jones/CAFOD
England

Prayer for Detained Asylum Seekers

Lord Jesus, you know how it feels to be a refugee;
to be rejected by your own flesh and blood;
to have no voice
                    no power
                        no home;
to be misunderstood, not heard.
In your love, Lord, have mercy on those
who turn to us for freedom but
find only a prison.
Have mercy also on us, for our failure to love
and give us the grace and compassion
to care for those whose lives are in danger
and who seek asylum in our land.
Through Jesus Christ our Lord.
Amen

Jesuit Refugee Service
United Kingdom

Woman, You are Called ...

You are Woman.

> You are woman –
> Strong soaring with wings far stretched into the horizon
> Reaching to the heights
> Bowing to the depths.

> You are woman –
> Strong – reaching out to other women and together –
> Discovering the depths of relationships
> With self
> With family
> With community with creation

> You are woman –
> Strong – learning and re-learning
> Shouting from the depths of your being
> the integrity of these relationships
> The profound insight that's
> Grounded in solid granite

Food embargo

Red lips,
White lips!

> Bright eyes,
> Dull eyes!

> > Rosy cheeks,
> > Pale cheeks!

Policies and decisions drawn in the board rooms,
        carpeted floors and air-conditioned rooms,
Along the street sits a woman tired and weak
Around her neck tiny arms embraced
        tiny hands outstretched
'A bowl of thin rice gruel, please, madam, sir!'
the voice trails on
the figures to invisibility.

Red lips
White lips!

> Bright eyes,
> Dull eyes!

Rosy cheeks,
Pale cheeks!

Tell me what is fair.
Tell me what is just.
Help me understand.

Bibiana Bunuan
Philippines/Tanzania/USA

The Age Old Excuse!

Churches are so full of people who excuse themselves from the mission and ministry of the church because they think they are too old.

You can't mean me:
 I'm too old,
  too tired,
   too weak
    to serve you now,
     my Lord.

You can't mean me:
 with aching bones,
  fading sight,
   trembling hands
    and wobbly legs,
     I'm too old,
      to serve you now.

You can't mean me:
 I've got no strength
  to break your bread
   pour your wine
    or kneel before you
     with a prayer
      and wash your feet.
       I'm too old, my Lord,
        to serve you now.

You can't mean me:
 I'm like a tree
  with falling leaves,
   its fruit all gone
    and ready for the barren months
     of winter time.
      It's too late, my Lord,
       for me to serve you now.

Forgive me if I laugh, but Lord:
 You can't mean me,
  I'm much too old
   to bring new life into the world.
    It's someone else you want,
     not me,
      I'm much too old
       to serve you now.

Richard Becher
England

Eternal Life Found in a Rubbish Bin

My father used to get drunk and abuse us constantly. My mother decided to flee to the city with only the clothes she stood up in, taking her children with her. With no money, no relations or friends, she arranged for a cellar for us to live in and her work as a domestic servant sustained us.

One day, my mother became sick and doctors could not diagnose what was wrong with her. She stayed in bed with her body paralysed and in great pain. My elder sister was seven at the time and she cooked for us until the food ran out. She went out with my brother to gather the remains of food from garbage bins. Together with the bones that she got from the butcher's, she made them into soup which did for all our meals. Every day it was the same story.

One day my sister gave my mother a little book and said, 'Look what I found in the garbage bin'. She wasn't to know that the book would change our lives forever. On that death bed, when our mother read the New Testament, Christ touched her life. Suddenly she got up, moved her legs and said, 'Jesus has cured me ... ' Nobody had ever knocked on our door to speak of Jesus, And with no one teaching her, she knelt and offered a prayer of thanks to God, asking forgiveness for her sins. She put her hand against my head and prophesied, 'This son of mine will live to speak of this book.'

God confirmed my mother's wish and at 25 years of age, I took on the role of being called to preach the gospel.

Daniel Elias Fernandades
Brazil

Dangerous Games
(Reading: Matthew 11:16–24)

What are you like?
asks Jesus
Squabbling children,
never content,
backs to each other,
ears shut
to each other's music.
Caught up in your games,
you expect God to play
by your rules,
adopt your standards.
No extremes:
not too outrageous,
not over cheerful,
nothing to disturb
your sheltered discontent.

God of wisdom and
understanding,
make us sensitive
to the mood music
of our time
its celebrations
and its sad laments,
its loud reality
and its plaintive call
for meaning.
Give us the energy to dance,
the tenderness to weep,
with your people,
as Jesus did.

Heather Pencavel
England

Lives are the Currency Spent in War's Carnage

Lives are the currency spent in war's carnage,
self-int'rest blinding the people in power.
Reckless decisions are made without wisdom;
God, through your love, hold us back from this hour.

Nation meets nation but language is twisted,
lies are clothed as truth, while ill poses as good;
all that now matters, it seems, is the victory
bought through the spilling of innocent blood.

God of the innocent, dying unheeded,
God of Gethsemane, Christ of the cross,
hear the world's pleading, then offer your loving,
hands scarred with nails reach to share in our loss.

Then in our dying, God bring resurrection,
lift us and save us, renew and forgive;
through devastation where meaning lies broken
bring us new love and a reason to live.

Tune: Stewardship
Andrew Pratt
England

My Mother in Heaven

Mother in Heaven,
paternity can only limit your grace.
To call you Mother God
shortens the distance between humanity and divinity.

I don't need a military Father God.
After studying about warfare,
I'm fed up with masculinity
The result is only violence!

Can we have a more civilised way
to sort out our conflicts?
Why do we have to use a gun,
to shoot and kill?

As a Mother
you know how to care and treasure life
You understand our feelings more truly
have sympathy on our emotion more deeply.
How can a father-image compare with your maternity?

You create life
you are the Mother of Eve
the Mother of our mothers
You know the price for just one single human being.
You cry if just a single one is lost and killed.

As I'm in despair
your comfort will stand by me
my sorrow and suffering
is your grief and agony.

Wong Mei Yuk
Hong Kong

Seven Happy Women

When asked how old she was, Wallian had no clear answer. She said maybe fifty or sixty. Wallian told us, 'I was born in Kullonda village and after my marriage I lived in Mundali village with my husband, our five children and my husband's family. Mundali and Kullonda villages are in the state of Uttar Pradesh, north-east India. We had a small piece of agricultural land there. To support the family I assembled necklaces brought by some unknown contractors. Twelve years ago, my husband died and life became difficult for us. I always believed in being self-dependent and did not want to depend on my sons, but women have to live with the sons' families, so I came to live with my eldest son in the suburbs of Delhi.

I found out about work opportunity at Tara * and joined the project three or four years ago. I did not want to be in the house all the time with my daughter-in-law and grand children. It was not very smooth going. I felt unhappy and found myself at their mercy. Once I came here I really liked it. It is good to be in the house but not the whole day. You have to understand it. I like to work and be useful.

I mainly do assembling work here with the help of small tools like a plastic cutter. I feel happy that I get my own money. I had to marry off my daughter. We did not have much money and my husband was not there anymore. My sons gave some money but it was not enough. So I saved money and made nearly half of the marriage expenses myself. It is a matter of satisfaction that my daughters are well settled now. Still I help my daughters from time to time. I do not have to ask my son for money.

There are seven women here and we are happy to be sharing our time together while working. We like to spend our day here. I am thankful to Traidcraft for the work given to us. We are thankful for the support and we hope to get more work in future.

* Background on Tara Projects

Tara Projects is a non-profit organisation based in Delhi, serving some 25 community-based groups of artisans from all regions in North India. They have been supplying Traidcraft for over 20 years and are currently Traidcraft's biggest supplier of crafts. Tara's objective is to help craft workers achieve self-sufficiency by providing income-generating opportunities and developing marketing skills. They have brought about major changes in these craft groups and their communities due to fair trade sales.

Traidcraft
England

I Want to Change the World

I want to change the world
says my sister
only half wry
and so do I
want to sanction
unholy
Monsanto
regreen '90 million hectares'
salvage the simple apple
as if
after this Fall
there can be
Spring.

Joanna Margaret Paul
Aotearoa New Zealand

To Change It All – for Good

A mess – this world. How depressing it gets.
News headlines
Emphasising the pain and horror of it all.
Good news, they say, is no news.

Are they right?
Just pause – consider how good news affects us.

Spirits lifted, hope restored
that it's worth going on,
worth the seemingly unending struggle
to change it all – for good.

Yes, for good – for good that is not 'evil'
               for good that is 'for ever'
Good news – God at work
Like a seed, split and broken
to give birth to abundant life.
Like yeast, bubbling into action
to re-form flour into bread.
Like a hidden treasure,
discovered when least expected.
Like a pearl,
found only through much effort in the searching.
Like a great catch of fish,
The good mixed in among the bad.

Good news –
there to be heard
     to be shared,
     to be lived –
To mend the mess – for good
             for God
   and all creation.

Wendy Ross-Barker
England

Living Our Difficult Days

(including items on illness, mental and physical impairments, hospitalisation,
rest and nursing home facilities, abuse and domestic violence, road accidents

**Illness, mental and physical impairments, hospitalisation,
rest and nursing home facilities**

Still Life

I went to see Elizabeth on Intensive Care
She looked very beautiful, very serene,
    like a statue carved in living tissue,
An angel in a trance.

O Lord, give her back to us, she's not an angel,
She's an ordinary human being –
Although I can see now how beautiful,
How very beautiful. I put my hand to touch her
It's hard because of all the wires and attachments
Where the hospital is holding her to itself
So I can hardly lay a finger on her anywhere.
Touch her yourself, Lord, I can't –

Touch Elizabeth. No ifs or buts,
Let your healing power give life to her mortal body,
Restore her senses and renew her mind,
    to love more deeply and love more truly
Than ever before. Do it Lord,
Do this amazing thing. As you raised your Son from the grave,
Raise Elizabeth now from this living death
And give her to herself and to us.

Roger Grainger
England

Echoes

Confused, alone she sat,
not deep in the chair, but on the edge of it.
Her fingers twisting in an endless circles
of emptiness.
Eyes seeing nothing we could follow.
Mind in a distant place beyond our reach.
No flicker of recognition or welcome
from the one who had cradled me,
nurtured me, waited eagerly for my step
inside the door each day.

Words were no use, we thought.
This was a bad day
and she would never know we had been there
watching the disintegration
of her fiery, independent spirit;
the slow loss –
although today she was gone from us already.

Elsewhere rustles of interest
told the arrival of the keyboard player
with tattered books of music
from a bygone age
and those who could, gathered in chattering flock
to finger-tap and listen.

And then, among melodies familiar with age,
came 'bright and beautiful' and 'creatures great and small,'
and a thin, clear voice from that lonely chair
joined in a chorus from some childhood time.
Life gave its echo back to us
and brought the tears.

Marjorie Dobson
England

Goodbye Van Gogh

You're not here again today are you, Nora;
not here in the frail body, cheeks more sunken.
'Where will you get a snake?'
'I don't want a snake, Nora.'
'You can get one in Sainsbury's –
they have them in there;
Cornelius, he was the victorious one.'

Where is the real you hiding?
You must be somewhere –
waiting in another dimension perhaps,
maybe Cornelius knows,
but your soul cannot unlock its own door.

We talk jabberwocky to each other.
No use reading you your favourite poems,
Eliot is wandering the waste landscape.
No use looking at books of art this time;
Van Gogh's is closed now,
Monsieur Roulin has shut the post office
and Vincent has gone with the crows.

Cecily Taylor
England

Shoe Laces

(for all people who live with and love through mental illness)

He stares
at his feet,
shoes loosely on,
laces hanging long and free.

He stares;
stares at his feet,
stares at his hands.
His mind confused
and numbed
and puzzled by the problem of not knowing,
of knowing that he should know,
knowing that he does know,
but knowing all too well
that now he doesn't know,
just doesn't know
how to tie his shoe laces
any more.

Executive decisions,
complicated strategies,
difficult manoeuvres
all once were his.

But now
he simply
cannot
tie his shoe laces.

The child in him
looks up at her through tear stained eyes,
his furrowed brow
wordlessly begging her,
pleading with her,
to understand
and help,
to rescue him.

She kneels before her child of sixty-one
and ties his laces,
dries his tears,
hugs him
and prays
that he will once again
walk tall.

Pat Marsh
England

Between Heaven and Earth

The waiting room can be a terrible place. It's bad enough waiting for the doctor when you are apprehensive about test results or the dentist as you can hear the drill on another patient.
The hospital waiting room must be one of the worst when someone is having an operation but more so when you are expecting a consultant to come with news of what can be done next, if anything, for someone you love.
When my wife was in a coma the 'waiting room' became both the place of hope and fear of what the doctor might say. It was in the waiting room that I realised the coma is a part of the journey where the boat is drifting on the ocean of life between the shores of heaven and earth.
While I wait in one place hoping for her safe arrival I could see God waiting on both shores ready to greet her wherever she arrived.

Do not be afraid
  as you drift on the ocean
    between the shores
      of heaven and earth.
The storm has calmed,
  the wind is still;
    the waters smooth,
      but soon your sails will billow
and speed you safely home
  where love waits to greet you
    on the shoreline of our lives
where new beginnings find their dawn.
So, do not be afraid
  as you drift on the ocean
between the shores of heaven and earth.

Jesus woke to calm your storm,
  and wind and waves obeyed,
    so do not lose your faith,
      do not fear calm or storm
for he still sits beside you
  preparing for the moment
    when the gentle breeze will blow
and with the tide you'll move
  until you step ashore again
    to be embraced by peace.
So, do not be afraid
  as you drift on the ocean
    between the shores of heaven and earth
for while we wait where we are
  God will meet you on either side.

Richard Becher
England

Not Knowing Anyone

Alone,
and just inside that crowded room,
I stood,
the Babel-babble conversation
roaring round me.
But I was edgy and bewildered,
unconnected.

Until, across the room
I heard my name –
not called,
but spoken of with knowledge –
and there was one, at least,
who recognised my being,
not my face.

It was enough.
Existing in her mind
she had enlivened me.
Now I could be a part
of those around.

I wonder –
did that woman ever know
how she had spoken me to life?

Marjorie Dobson
England

Diagnosis

I attended the clinic at half-past two
The doctor shook my hand said pleased to meet you
I hear your memory isn't so good
My heart started pounding
I knew that it would
He asked questions about my life
Whether my childhood was happy and nice
Could I remember the start of the war
And the date it finished
I said I couldn't because I wasn't sure
Could I count backwards
From a hundred in sevens
Also forward this time in elevens
I tried to do the best I could
But my memory's not so good.

The doctor asked me to wait in the room
Said he would be back very soon.
I sat there thinking, what could it be
When he came back in the room to me
I've talked to my colleague
And we know what's wrong.
Your brain isn't working
As it did when you were young.
We have some bad news, I'm sorry to say
You have been diagnosed with having Alzheimer's today.
Could be a year, or maybe two
Before it affects you, a lot more than it does
We will give you medication
To keep you stable
Your husband will look after you
As long as he's able
Try not to worry or get upset
You still have a few more years yet.

Margaret Alford
England
Via Alzheimer's Society/Living with Dementia Project

Spiral Staircase

A friend called the other day
I said have you heard the news
I'm about to go on a journey
But it's not a flight or a cruise
It's down a spiral staircase
Three or four steps at a time
But I shall have to watch myself
That I don't slip or slide
If I hold on the rails tightly
And focus straight ahead
I won't have to face the darkness
Maybe I'll face hope instead.

She stared at me and finally said
I don't know what you're saying.
Under my breath she doesn't know
How hard that I am praying.
I have something to tell you
We think it right to know
I have an illness
It's invasive and quite slow.

She held my hands, my knees felt weak
So full up, I could hardly speak.
'Now dry your eyes, no more tears
We have been friends for many years.
Both had our share of happiness and sorrow
Remember it could be a new beginning tomorrow.
So I'll help you through this awful thing
You are strong my dear friend
I know you will fight and not give in'.

Margaret Alford
England

Snowbound

She gazed across the scene of glistening white,
no mark to show that life had wandered by,
for all that had been vanished in the night,
swept underneath the carpet from the sky.
Smiling a thousand, thousand thoughts away,
the sun shone weakly through the bowing trees,
its beauty barred, the brightness of the day
held fast by soulless shadowed fantasies.
Fragmented and cast down before her eyes,
it gave way to the clouds of her despair
and icy nature gripped her tears and sighs,
defying her to make her footprints there.
So hope lay frozen in its earthbound cold,
for only love can step when fear takes hold.

Colin Ferguson
England

Meet Sam, aged 14

Sam has muscular dystrophy which means that now he uses a wheelchair and no longer has much use of his hands and legs. He drives his wheelchair with a small control panel. Sam likes school and is good at maths. He says:

'I'm interested in computers and football. I support Liverpool and I like playing with my Playstation. I have one good friend at home and when he comes round we play computers and go to the park.

The other kids near where I live are nasty. I just ignore them. They call you names and things like that. I ignore them because they're little kids about nine and ten and they don't hurt me that much. There's one who is a bit older. He's about twelve. He just does it because he doesn't like me, that's all.

I think some gadget shops are quite hard to get into because they're so full of stuff. Once I got caught on a shelf and I knocked everything over and everybody just looked at me and didn't help. They just stared at me. Stupid isn't it? Mum had to pick them up all by herself.

I remember once we went to a holiday camp. I was allowed on this ride. It was like one of those ships that swing up and down. I was allowed on it five or six times and then, all of a sudden, another man said I couldn't go on it. He said "if you can't walk you can't go on". That's why we left. We just went back home and we haven't been there since.

And one other thing, I'm sick of people going into disabled parking places without a disabled badge. It makes us go to a far away space and have to walk'.

John Grooms
England

Tom's Problem

Tom White is a normal teenager with lots of friends. He is good at school work and keen on sport. The only slightly unusual thing about Tom is that he has been diabetic since he was nine. To control his condition he gives himself insulin injections every day.

Being a diabetic means that the level of sugar in his blood is not properly controlled by the body. If it drops badly, it can cause dizziness and make the muscles stiffen up (this is called a 'hypo'). When this occurs, the body needs to take in some sugar quickly. If this does not happen, the sufferer can pass out. In February 2000, Tom went on a school skiing trip to Austria. During the trip, Tom had a serious hypo shortly after waking up one morning. This was the first time Tom had had a hypo with so little warning.

On returning to England, the teachers decided that they would not allow Tom to go on any future school trips.

'Obviously, I was pretty disappointed when I was told I couldn't go,' says Tom. 'We were meant to be going canoeing, kayaking and sailing.'

Tom's parents got in touch with the school, but the school refused to talk about the issue.

John Grooms
England

Dream or Nightmare?

Mr Boyce was sixty-five and for his birthday his children gave him and his wife a voucher costing £149.00 for a trip to a top London theatre and a four-star hotel. Mrs Boyce uses a wheelchair and is blind. When they phoned to confirm the booking both the hotel and the theatre said they had no access for people with disabilities.

The company that sold the voucher had no information about access for people with disabilities. They offered Mr and Mrs Boyce a different show (a musical, not a play) and a two-star hotel.

Mrs Boyce said: 'They made me feel like a second-class citizen'.

John Grooms
England

DMDs?
(A very special day)

Today is my birthday. The sun always shines on my birthday. It's raining.

I can't go out today. Not because my legs are too stiff or too wobbly, not because vertigo has overtaken me once again, not even because I don't know where I've put the car keys. I can't remember when I last felt so well, so alive.

I have to stay home to accept my first delivery of 'Disease Modifying Drugs'.

My last chance, my hope for the future.

Today my sunshine will be delivered in a box.

Liz Burns
England
Via Multiple Sclerosis Society

Brought Through
(A Prayer of Thanksgiving after a Hysterectomy)

From the pouring-out of my life-blood,
from the fierce dragging weight in my body,
I have been brought through
to a place of safety and rest.

Through the skilled hands of the surgeon,
and the caring attentiveness of nurses,
I have been surrounded by love
and give thanks for all that is.

From the terror of being abandoned to pain
and the fear of vulnerable helplessness,
I have been brought through
to a place of safety and rest.

Through a cocoon of friendship and prayer
and women's hands that touch and heal,
I have been surrounded in love,
and give thanks for all that is.

In the gentleness of rest,
in the renewal of energy and trust,
I open to this flow of love
and give thanks to all that is.

Jan Berry
England

Depression

Is this an empty plate?

Only shadows lodge here.
Their souls do not twitch to see
corncrakes in frilly meadows,

Homing rooks and
Frost-split stones in ice's trickle.
Here glory has slipped away.

We are not attuned to
a green awakening of sorrel,
barley grass in the lea field,

lulling catkins,
the rainbow geese
and what is magnified by silence.

We are unfixed, uncaught
by the snap of the known,
and signposted.

We have not danced
by the unstaying sea
or aspired to silent prayers.

We are absent, forgotten,
unsettled at unloving
in human hearts and afraid.

This is an empty place,
only senseless shadows
lodge here.

Derek Webster
England

Fling Wide My Door
(written while recovering from depression)

I have a longing
to scrub my floor,
to polish my windows
and paint the door.

To furnish my rooms
with simple things
until they echo with laughter
and my heart sings.

In my garden the Light
will envelop my soul
mind, body and spirit
one integral whole.

I should throw open
my gate and my door
to the cold and the hungry
and the victims of war.

I could hold them and heal them
and nourish them so,
from that river of love
Which will soon overflow –

For there at its mouth
lies a boulder so great
that if I cannot shift
will crack open my heart.

So Creative Spirit, come
flow with the stream
of conscious endeavour
to fulfil my dream.

Yes, I have a yearning
to spring-clean my floor,
to make sparkle my windows
and fling wide my door!

Celia Snaith
England

Face to Face

I met her yesterday ...
inwardly weeping .
You could tell ...
the depression weighed heavily.
Conscious of the lone silence ...
she spoke to break the barrier of pain.

I prayed ...
for the Spirit's anointing.
To refresh and renew ...
mysteriously as morning dew.

Treasure the developing space –
To be free;
To become.

Simply draw up a chair,
Share – face to face
With the One
In whose image you're made.

Dig deep;
Hold nothing back;
In times of doubt and stress
It's good to talk, watch, wait and listen
To one who knows you well and longs
to bless
While you prepare for ultimate
wholeness – given.

Wendy Whitehead
England

The Birthday

There was a woman in a corner
of the labour ward
cut off by screens and grief
and being near I could hear her weeping.

Later when the screens parted a little
we talked between the waves that sought me
or rather it was she who spoke:
My little baby girl –
the cord was round her neck –
they could do nothing.

She made an effort then to gain control:
I must be grateful though –
I have four lovely boys.

Thus she attempted to heave off
the years of hoping
the months of waiting
the lifeline turned to noose.

Why did they leave her there
beside that room
where cries of new-live babies
ripped her heart?

That was some years ago
and still I cannot forget
for part of me went home with her
to know those empty arms
beside the vacant cot.

Now when my son blows out his years
I see her somewhere
trying not to count
invisible and unlit candles;
I see her
silent
wondering.

Cecily Taylor
England

How Long, O God
(A psalm of lament during illness)

How long must I struggle with weariness
Before joy and energy return?
How long must I search for healing
Before I can rejoice in my strength?

Wait in trust and gentleness:
Hope on the God within
For her breath will restore you.

Where is the spark of vitality
Which fired my joy and laughter?
Where is that passion to create
Which nurtured my energy with vision?

Wait in trust and gentleness:
Hope on the God within
For her breath will restore you.

How long must I protect myself
Before I feel safe to give freely?
How long before I go again with the crowd
My heart rejoicing in the laughter of friends?

Wait in trust and gentleness:
Hope on the God within
For her breath will restore you.

Jan Berry
England

A Crisis in Hospital

Lord Jesus Christ,
in weakness I am yours
in fear I am yours
in darkness I am yours.

You know it all.
See me through
and bless me.

Bernard Thorogood
Australia

Trust

I know I'll be alright if I just do
What doctor said.
I must remember to try and always do
What doctor said.
When I start to feel it coming on, all I have to do
Is what she said.
Hold tight, concentrate, think hard, I must do
What doctor said.

I'd be alright now, if I could only remember what it was
Doctor said.

Roger Grainger
England

Safety

This place is huge. It's more immense
Than the sum of parts, as exhaustive as imagination.
I hug its lovely vastness to myself
And feel it pressing me together – no chance here
Of getting lost. Where you can distinguish landmarks
That's where you get lost.

This place is bigger than I thought it was. It's wider
Than my thinking, like my feeling
It goes on forever, growing more intense, more authentic.
I see myself running from ward to ward, screaming.
Cannoning from corner to corner, breaking down doors.
Careering to the centre and the centre's centre.
Screaming.

Maybe tomorrow, Meanwhile this place is huge –
And it's me.

Roger Grainger
England

Not That Easy

My first reaction
on reaching the ward
was one of
pure breath-stopping panic.
This wasn't a ward
in which you recovered
it was a place
where you waited to die.

No-one spoke
no-one was able to.
The only sound was moaning
or occasional 'Oh God'
and the lady in the corner bed
looked like she was praying.

I went to the bathroom.
Dirty clothes and bed linen
lay in the base of the shower
urine seeped from them
and now covered the floor.
I walked through it slipping by the door
and my slippers were wet.

The next day
A priest was brought
to the lady in the corner bed.
They prayed urgently together.
Her son told me
she longed for death
but said bitterly
'It's not that easy to die'.

I went home on the third day.
I looked around
and said goodbye
but no-one answered.
They didn't realise I'd been there.
I threw my slippers in the bin
on the way out.

Geoffrey Herbert
England

What Am I Waiting For?

How much longer am I going to have to wait here like this, I wonder?
Sister said 'round about three o'clock'. Well, it's
Four now and they haven't come yet.
I do wish they'd be quick:
They should be bringing the old lady back soon,
I should think. They took her down to the theatre soon after lunch.
– not that we had any lunch, of course, being down for tests this afternoon –
I feel so stupid, lying here in this absurd flannel night shirt ...
Oh, why don't they come!

Just listen to me, Lord, carrying on as usual
I can't think why I'm going on like this,
It isn't as if it was a serious operation.
It isn't as if I had anything to be frightened about.
Just routine tests – they must have done hundreds of them.
Thousands of them. (Oh why don't they come!)

He joked about it himself: said he'd 'never lost a patient from this one'
He was joking, of course.
So it's absolutely stupid for me to be frightened.

And I'm not frightened, of course
Not a bit.

But I wish they'd come.

Roger Grainger
England

On a Diagnosis of Asperger's Syndrome

Is it bad news, Bringer of Good?
Is it bad news that he is who he is
Rather than making a hash of being somebody else?

Is it bad news that the end of a parent's tether
Can be the start of a new lead?

Or that the anger you thought a good parent should enlist
Is a burden you don't have to pick up, for now.
A relief, to concentrate on patience instead?

Is it bad news that not coping is coping after all
And that one more barrier of my own prejudice is shaken at its roots
Because love won't permit it?

And where barriers crumble
Our unaccountable God
– Good News –
is at work.

David Coleman
Scotland

Balthazaar

(to a partially sighted child, drawing)

Spread-eagled on the floor,
his body taut and thin,
stretched across the page he tore
from the flip-chart,
in order to draw
his King.

At first it seemed
as if it were the tip of his nose
doing the drawing, when
from beneath his chin emerged
the small fist, tightly closed
over the fat felt marker pen,
his ally in art.

His eyes beguiled by such
a cunning hand, from which,
with short swift strokes
the black lines flew, circled,
diverged and drew together,
over and over again –
finally to disclose
the dancing forms of Balthazaar,
with glorious heraldry.
In size and shape
from top to toe
just as the page
decreed.

This partially-sighted child
of seven
should surely grow
to be a man of vision who,
like Baltahazaar of old,
will so bestow upon the earth
such gifts as are indeed
of golden worth.

Celia Snaith
England

Loss of Sight

How useless I feel, Lord,
now that I can no longer see properly.

For me there are no more eyes meeting across a crowded room,
no more sideways glances to convey intimacy,
no more sharing the joke by the twitch of the lips,
no more reading the truth by the averted gaze,
no more recognising a friend from a distance.

Now I stand alone
waiting for the sensitive ones
to identify themselves and engage me –
while others wonder why I never speak
to them.
Little do they know
how often I thought I did,
only to embarrass a stranger.

Lord, it is so hard,
when I have grown accustomed to the seeing world,
to find myself no longer there.

Help me to persevere
in finding ways of coping.
Help me to be patient
in my dealings with those who do not understand.
Console me in my loss of dignity
and in my reluctance to be dependant on others.
Restore the soul of my independence,
by teaching me new ways of self-reliance
and by using skills, which are not affected
by my sight-impairment,
to be of service to others.

Lord, my life is still yours.
Help me to follow this confusing direction
with hope and confidence in You.

Marjorie Dobson
England

You Disturb Me

Where are You, Lord?

Where exactly are You
In the suffering and pain
Of this cruel, frightening world?

Sometimes, Lord,
Sometimes You really disturb my faith.

It's not that I don't believe
That You're a God of infinite, perfect love,
I do. At least, I'm trying to.
It's simply that I just
Don't understand.

It's not difficult to see You
In the radiance of a summer flower,
To sense You in the glorious artistry
Of a sunset sky.
Far harder to figure out
How to see Your hand
In the wretched squalor of the poor
Or, worse still, the distended bellies
Of the hungry, starving.

Gazing on the wonder of a new born babe,
I marvel at your gifts.
But looking on the fear and pain
Within a cancer riddled body,
I ask myself
Where?
Where are You then?

Are you at work behind the scared eyes
Of the frightened refugee,
The misery of the homeless, alcoholic tramp;
Are you active in the tragedy
Of the AIDS patient,
Or the drug addict barely out of school?

Where are You then, Lord?
It's then,
Yes it's then, that I don't quite
Understand.
It's then that
You disturb me, God.

Pat Marsh
England

Abuse and Domestic Violence

In Situations of Abuse

God, I feel so alone, so cut off, so shut out. I can't relate to you as 'Lord', 'Almighty Father', Eternal King'. I can't cope with your power and authority as I have none. I am frightened of your otherness, but as Jesus, loving friend who valued those who were shut out, who was condemned and tortured himself, I can approach you. As Holy Spirit who cuddles us to her breast, who inspires us with courage I can approach you.

Please hold me tight; heal my broken body and battered spirit. Empower me with the knowledge of your love and belief so that I may learn to value that I am made in your image and worth so much more that I dare contemplate.

I pray for strength to love myself enough to leave the abuse. I ask that you bring the reality of the resurrection into my life, that your fire and joy will blossom into a new life of love, justice, hope and peace.
Amen

Zam Walker
Wales/Scotland

The Ballad of Maria Colwell

The first case of child abuse which caused an enormous public outcry was in the 1970s. Lessons were to be learnt. Sadly through the years there have been other horrific cases.

Oh where has young Maria gone – why did she leave so soon?
The snowdrops and the daffodils upon her grave were strewn;
They called a Court Inquiry then of how she came to die –
Three people sat for nine long weeks and asked the question: Why?
The waves flowed up, the waves flowed down as still they flow today;
The searching waves turned up the stones and time flowed on its way.

For nine long weeks they searched for truth with those who touched her life,
Who phoned the NSPCC, who feared a violent knife;
With those who did not learn the facts, with those who heard her cry;
A hundred thousand pounds was spent to find the reason why.
The waves flow up, the waves flow down – what is it that they say?
The searching waves turn up the stones and time flows on its way.

She had a happy foster home and lived there five glad years,
And when she had to go back home she screamed and fought with tears;
But still the law moved on its course, though later in reply
It questioned three score folk and ten to find the reason why.
The waves flow up, the waves flow down, not many more must flow
Before we alter what we must in view of all we know.

A lot of people tried to help, so why did things go wrong
When home is where your heart is and it's there that you belong?
And if we pause to question it these facts can now supply
Some fifteen hundred thousand pleading words to tell us why.
The waves flow up, the waves flow down, the waves call out her name;
The flowing waves can't wash our hands – we all must share the blame.

Cecily Taylor
England

Time

A time to grieve for what could have been,
A time to cry for what should have been,
Childhood innocence snatched away
No chance for fun and childish play.
No security in love
No reassuring cuddles and hugs.
Alone, afraid but cannot cry,
Hide fear and pain so deep inside.
Life is gone existence is here
Struggling and surviving in fear,
Wanting to die yet longing to live
Knowing that life has so much to give.
God's reaching out His hand so near
My only chance is to face my fear
Grasp God's hand and hold it tight
Through the darkness of my night.
Dawn approaches morning has come
The time to live my new life has begun.

N Stevenson
England

Tears

The tears want to fall but I can't let go. I need to be in control. For too long now
my life has not been my own. Now I am safe – surrounded by my own personal
barriers built high and strong to keep everyone away so I will never be hurt
again. But I do still hurt. The pain is inside – some buried so deep I cannot even
recall the nightmare events that caused it to be born in me. I am lonely, I want
to feel safe and belong, be accepted, be healed and whole again. To achieve that
I need to let go – to let the tears wash the barriers away, to let the tears water
the dry, parched ground of my soul to bring life to my existence and let me
grow as the child God made me to be.

N Stevenson
England

Fear

My fear holds the strings that control my life, making me move as it wills.
Tightening the strings on my emotions and feelings, refusing to let me be free.
The spirit inside longs to soar and be free – free to worship, free to live, free to
breathe without fear. As I've graduated from existence to survival to life, I want
my soul to be alive too – not being held hostage with fear as the tormentor.
Torturing me day and night, pulling me anyway it wills. I tell my torturer God
hasn't given me a spirit of fear, I speak the language of logic, my fear does not.
It hates the church and any talk of God and punishes me profusely if I over step
the line it paints to keep me away from its dislikes. I try to fight for my freedom
but the exertion drives me further into my prison. Now I am learning a new
language – the language of perfect love. My fear cannot compete with that for
it is too powerful and can break the chains my fear used to hold me captive.
This new language takes time for me learn, time for me to accept and believe
I can use it but slowly, link by link, the chain of fear is being broken forever.

N Stevenson
England

Soaring Wings and Strengthened Dreams (1)

Leader: 'I have come that they may have life, and may have it in all its
fullness'. (John 10:10b)

Hymn: **Lord God, Your Love Has Called Us Here** (Hymns and Psalms 500)

Prayer of Thanksgiving and Confession

Leader: Creator God, we come today thankful for all that is good and beautiful;

For trees and flowers in all their diversity
For mountain grandeur and the soft peacefulness of woodland streams.
For good and wholesome relationships in which people are equal partners,
For pockets of stillness amid the hustle and bustle of everyday life.

But we also come today aware of what is wrong in our world:

Of relationships that are violent and abusive,
Of people who seem to find gain in the suffering of others,
Of those who refuse to listen to the abused,
Of those who turn the other way when unfair treatment is meted out.

Forgive us, O God, for all our failings.

Our God hears and forgives. In silence we offer them to you.

May we listen to the voices of those around us and work towards transforming relationships, attitudes and structures, so that men and Women may live in peace and harmony.

We pray in the name of our Lord Jesus Christ. Amen

Reader: Living with Violence. Emma's Story

We went to church as usual on Sunday. My husband was directing the singing and leading the prayers. He's a pillar of the church and respected as a spiritual and pastoral leader. John says my place is with the children, so I help with the 5 – 7 years-olds in Sunday School. It was a long service and the children got very restless. It was hard to keep them interested and occupied.

John had people to see after the service so I had to walk home. He won't let me drive his car. Hannah, our two year-old was tired so I had to carry her nearly all the way. Paul in his push chair was crying; his dirty nappy making him sore. It was a quarter to one when we got home. I hadn't prepared the vegetables but I had to see to Paul. So, when John drove up, the dinner wasn't nearly ready. He began shouting at me. He'd been busy about the Lord's work, giving out to other people; I'd only been with the children and any fool could do that, yet I still hadn't managed to get the dinner for one o'clock. He went into the lounge to read the Baptist Times.

After he'd said grace, we ate. He criticised my cooking because the carrots were still hard and it was Angel Delight again for pudding; his mother always made apple pie for Sunday lunch and she didn't have all the gadgets I did. When I'd done all the washing up and put the children down for their rest, I lay down on the bed and sobbed from exhaustion and guilt and shame at my incompetence. However, hard I try I can never win John's approval.

After a while he came and found me; he needed a shirt ironed and ready for the evening service. He shook me hard to make me pull myself together. He's careful not to hurt me where it shows. He said I wasn't a good Christian wife; I wasn't giving him my full support as he did God's work.

That night, as usual, he made .love to me and then fell asleep straight away. I wish I could sleep. Night after night I lay awake, my body aches with weariness and the pain where he hits me. People look up to us a model of a Christian family; but I don't know how much longer I can cope.

Silence

Bible Reading: Mark 5: 25 – 34

Song: A Touching Place (Iona Community – Wild Goose Publications)

Reflection on the Bible Reading

Reader: A Story of Hope. Helen's Story

For years my husband beat me and I used to think 'perhaps I deserve to be treated like that – if I had behaved differently – if I'd tried harder – understood more'. But when it happened to my daughter who did react differently, I began to realise that it was not as simple as that. After years of crying, trying to talk to people without giving the real story and just coping as best I could, it is hard to describe the feeling of relief when the minister accompanied me to the solicitor. That was just the beginning of a long, slow process of healing which is still going on and which perhaps always will but is nevertheless a steady process which includes both therapy from a professional counsellor and years of being assured of God's love shown by a few very special people.

It has been hard to learn to believe in myself, to know that I am loveable, to have confidence in myself, to respond to God's calling to be a minister, a process which has involved a long process of selection and training. However, that has happened and although the struggle to love and believe in myself still goes on, I know that there is a resurrection, that there are folk out there who really can and want to help, and I know that God is using my past experience - with all its pain and struggles – to give life and hope to others. From what people say to me, what really helps them from my story is that, although the struggle goes on, there is hope and there is resurrection – but like many people who experience resurrection, it happens so slowly, almost imperceptibly at first, but very steadily and beautifully.

Song: Will You Come and Follow Me

Leader: An Act of Confession and Reconciliation *

Women who escape from abusive relationships find themselves piecing together the remains of their shattered lives. It is the responsibility of us all, men and women alike, to help people rebuild their lives after such devastation.

In this act of reconciliation you will have the opportunity to commit yourself to the rebuilding of broken lives through the placing of a broken piece of crockery at the cross. In doing so, we bring to the cross of Christ those, who like him, suffer at the hands of violent people. We stand in solidarity with women and indeed all victims of violence who are piecing their lives together. We involve ourselves in the process of re-creation of all God's people as we affirm the women who are recreating themselves.

Song: The Love of God Comes Close ('Wild Goose Songs' Wild Goose Publications)

Prayers of Intercession (for three voices)

One: We come together to listen and hear the voices of women who have experienced violence. We pray that God will help us to see beyond the respectable façade and see their need.

Two: Domestic violence only happens in working class families

Three: Domestic violence affects people from differing social groups, regardless of age, class, culture and religion. It is less often reported by those who are affluent.

One: Loving God, help us to support women who experience violence from those they are close to and help us to listen and believe them.

Response: Grant soaring wings and strengthened dreams

Two: Domestic violence doesn't happen in Christian homes.

Three: Christian homes are not immune. Even ministers and church leaders have been known to abuse their partners. Their respected position and the church structures often protect them.

One: Loving God, help us to listen to women who have experienced abuse from those in authority and have broken their position of trust.

Response: Grant soaring wings and strengthened dreams

Two: 'I don't abuse her, I just have a go at her and tell her she's stupid and always wrong'.

Three: Anyone who puts another person down, who is constantly belittling them is committing abuse.

One: Loving God, help each of us in our dealings with those close to us to treat them as we ourselves would wish to be treated, with encouragement and respect.

Response: Grant soaring wings and strengthened dreams

Two: If it were that bad she would leave.

Three: Women stay because of threats, enforced isolation, lack of money and hoping he will change.

One: Loving God, help us to support women who experience violence, so that they can have confidence to make informed choices about their lives.

Response: Grant soaring wings and strengthened dreams

Two:　　Loving God, may all of us, women and men alike, enjoy relationships built on respect and mutual trust. May each of us know peace, joy and fulfilment in our lives together.

In Jesus name we pray.
Amen

Hymn:　　**Lord Thy Church on Earth is Seeking** (Hymns and Psalms 774)

Leader:　　O God,
Where hearts are fearful and confined:
Grant freedom and daring.
Where anxiety is infectious and widening:
Grant peace and reassurance.
Where impossibilities close every door and window:
Grant imagination and resistance.
Where distrust shapes every understanding:
Grant healing and transformation.
Where spirits are daunted and dimmed:
Grant soaring wings and strengthened dreams.

The blessing of God, Creator, Redeemer and Sustainer be with us all.
Amen.

- **Confession and Reconciliation**

Preparation: *You will need to commit an act of violence to prepare for this part of the worship by smashing some old crockery. It is suggested that it is put in plastic bags and hit with a hammer so that there is no flying debris. There needs to be enough broken pieces so that each member of the congregation has a piece. Warn people to take care with the harp edges. Broken crockery is a powerful image of the violence that is experienced in the home.*

As members of the congregation will be asked to put together their pieces in the shape of a cross you will need a pencil outline of the cross on paper. The size of the cross will vary depending on the size of the congregation and the size of the broken crockery pieces that will make the mosaic.

As people come forward ask them to begin to create the mosaic by following the outline of the cross and work towards the centre. Remember that in a mosaic the pieces do not fit together perfectly. At the close of worship the crockery pieces may be glued (using a strong household glue) to the paper and displayed as a more permanent reminder of our standing in solidarity with women who are victims of domestic violence.

It is easier to move to music. During the piecing together of the mosaic it is suggested that people may like to sing to quiet music from Taize or the Iona

Community. The movement will happen much more comfortably if one or two people are prepared to make the first moves.

Frances Biseker
The Baptist Union of Great Britain
Women's Network of the Methodist Church, England
Keri Wehlander, Canada

Soaring Wings and Strengthened Dreams (2)

O God, where hearts are fearful and limited:
Grant freedom and daring.
Where anxiety is infectious and widening:
Grant peace and reassurance.
Where impossibilities close every door and window:
Grant imagination and resistance.
Where distrust reshapes every understanding:
Grant healing and transformation.
Where spirits are daunted and dimmed:
Grant soaring wings and strengthened dreams

Keri Wehlander
Canada

Losing the Fairytale

Small girl, big dreams of one day finding love
Abandonment, abuse and pain suffocate her like a glove
Being taught God is love yet the love she feels is pain
Breaks the silence punishment follows – silence reigns again.

Small girl grows, so does the fear of being hurt again
Yet for love she still craves but the love she finds brings pain
The dreams have died; nothing left just emptiness inside
Afraid to move, afraid to cry, I dare not feel, just want to hide.

Trust lies shattered on the ground
Hope lies silent there is no sound
Through the despair God brings his love
Surrounding, protecting me like a glove.

God has patience, without any measure
What we see as rubbish He knows is treasure
Slowly but surely He rebuilds me again
A glimpse of a rainbow through the darkness of pain.

Unconditional love he pours out to me
Soothing and calming no pain now, I'm free!
The small girl's fairytale is dead and gone
But I'm living a new life and I'm moving on

N Stevenson
England

The Journey

I am a victim
The pain that burns into my memory
The bruises that break my belief in life
The words that cut my trust into millions of pieces
Trying to be good enough yet failing again and again.

Alone in a prison of safety
Isolated in a noisy members only club
Grieving for a lost dream, a lost life
The remains of a shattered past contained in a black bin liner
A clash of cultures and life-styles threaten to engulf me
Wishing on a star for the nightmare to end
Awakening after a long dark night depressed
        to find I face the struggle of another day
Looking for an end to find it is only a beginning.

The beginning of a war to reclaim what is rightfully mine
An opinion, a sense of self-worth, self confidence
        and the chance to have a life –
A life worth living
A time of learning, of taking risks
Learning to trust, to make choices, to take responsibility
To put down all the guilt, all the pain
Let go of the hatred and self-loathing
Grasp my second chance with both hands
And thank God
I am a survivor.

N Stevenson
England

Tenderness and Violence
(written after hearing a talk about domestic violence)

Tenderness and violence:
a tangled web we weave;
though sharing fellowship in God
we practised to deceive.

The love we should have shared,
polluted in its course,
has been distorted, twisted, torn,
and I have no recourse.

O God, please set me free,
despite the vows I've made.
I need your love, you know my hurt,
I long to be re-made.

So take me as I am,
alone and scarred by pain,
and by your spirit heal, restore
that I might love again.

Andrew Pratt
England

The 'Me' In Conflict

Caught up
In the crossfire
Of the conflict which surrounds me.
Nerves
Razor sharp,
On a knife edge of tension.
Mind
Tightly curled
Into a taut defensive ball.
Knotted up.
Afraid.
Trembling
On the threshold
Of the precipice of fear.
Blinded by the hatred
Into thinking God has gone.
Why?
Why God?
Why?

Pat Marsh
England

Separation and Divorce

On My Own

All I wanted in life
is to stay with my wife
and now that she's gone
I cannot go on.
You meant so much to me
and that will always be.
Wish I could turn back time
to where we had a good time
it was nineteen-ninety-three
when you started to love me.
You have a heart of gold
and don't ever have to be old.
Eleven months we've been apart
and all that time it's ripped me apart.
How long does it take for a tear to dry?
I know I can't wait so long, no matter how I try.

The other day I was waiting for a bus
when I broke down in tears.
A guy came up to me to ask if I was OK
but I told him to go away
and began to cry even more.
He put his hands on my hands
said 'Come on, I'll take you to St Anne's.
After six months my pain was getting smaller
and my confidence keeps getting better.
Everyone around is so kind
but I admit my wife is still on my mind.
I'm so glad I had Mick there to help me
and others who came up to me.
I feel much easier going home
knowing I'll be able to make it on my own.

Matthew Everitt
St George's Crypt, Leeds, England

Separation or Divorce

It takes two to tango, to make a marriage.
Does it take two to break a marriage?

It's absolutely plain,
there is a guilty party.
I did my best, worked hard,
gave myself, was faithful,
        a homebuilder.
But I can't face that betrayal
at breakfast everyday.
It's absolutely plain,
there is a guilty party.

Did you understand?
Were you alert to silent despair?
Did you know what an irritant you were?
Perhaps you nagged too often
        or spoke too harshly
        or demanded too much
        or perhaps you were just too perfect
        for this messy marriage business.

So, dear God, I face my humanity,
        flawed as ever.
But you are healing and hope;
don't let me sink into chronic bitterness;
be with me in loneliness;
mend my heart, rekindle my love;
help me to being again.

Bernard Thorogood
Australia

Camera Shot

How long will it be, I wonder,
before you stop drifting
across the forefront of my thoughts?

Like a bit part actor
who seeks to be noticed for a bigger role,
it seems is if
you are constantly
wandering into camera shot
inside my mind.

I am trying to let you go,
move on,
begin again.

Please

stop wandering

into my mind.

I do not have a role for you
any more,
except in my memory archives.

Pat Marsh
England

Something To Do With Fire

Was it the wrong box of matches
or the damp weather
hindered the kindling
of this natural fire,
or that their mental indentations
did not lock together,
or an erratic balance
of desire?

Now there is little gain
in search or inquest,
enough to bear of pain
that each must live
with double emptiness;
for him the wanting,
for her the void
of what he could not give.

Cecily Taylor
England

No-one

Waking up.
All alone.
Sometimes that's the hardest time.

No-one to stir me
from the heaviness of slumber
into the wakefulness the day requires.

No-one to share a cuppa:
that first essential brew,
part of the ritual that helps me cross the border
from sleepiness
to the beginnings of the day.
No-one to nudge me if I'm late
or take his turn
to make that cup of tea.

No gently breathing 'other' one
beside me in the bed,
going through the same yawning struggle
of trying to break the bonds of sleep
and readjust to morning.

No hug. No kiss.
No competition for the loo.
No early morning chit-chat.
No-one to help me plan the format of my day,
draw out forgotten details
from my gently dozing memory.

No-one to break the silence.

Waking up.

Alone.

Sometimes that's the hardest time.

Pat Marsh
England

Foothills

Climbing up the foothills
of recovery
from the bottom
of the chasm of my grief
the darkness
of the valley of my pain
is flooded
with a soft diffusing light
as a new beginning
dawns
within my heart.

Your leaving me
has put me where I did not choose to be

but now I see
your loss has set me free.

Pat Marsh
England

When Parents Separate

What a mess!
What an awful mess!
You'd think grown-ups could run things better,
could make a life together,
could just keep going and keep the home.
But no, they just can't agree.
I've heard bitter words
which they think I can't hear.

Now I shall have to share out my time,
so much here and so much there,
like changing hotels,
and that's not my idea of home.

But it's not all bad,
for I think they still love me
in their funny way.

They cried, God, and I cried too,
but now it has happened,
give us some peace and some laughter.
Help us to heal the sore places,
so the bitterness doesn't last forever.

And, God, they used to tell me to grow up;
but I don't want to end in their kind of fight.
Perhaps growing up takes all life long.

Bless this house, O Lord, I pray,
Keep us always in your way;
    If I'm lonely night or day
    May your peace come in and stay.

Bernard Thorogood
Australia

Survival

Ride the wave, you said,
ride, float
let the tide carry you.

Don't fight the current
use your strength to guide
propel you on.

You ought to know
having survived a hurricane
that could have left you done.

Ride the wave, you said, *ride,*
only the resisting clinging one
finds himself battered
left most shattered.

Accepting,
you took the only thing
that mattered with you –
how you felt inside.

Cecily Taylor
England

The Other Side of Me

Plucking up the courage
To dare
To trust the cease-fire.
Conscious of incisions
Which though superficially healed
Are still a source of
Pain
So unforgiving in its rawness.

Kneeling
In the silence.

Making every agonising wound
Into a prayer.

I sense His soft anointing.
I hear Him say
'my child, I know.
I too have walked that path.
Come, share my crown of thorns
And let me love you
Into wholeness.'

Pat Marsh
England

Victims of Road Accidents

Prayers for Road Victims and Their Families

Let us hold before God those whose lives have ended prematurely through violent death on our roads and footways.

> Young children with whole lives before them crucially cut off
> Young men, most vulnerable of all to avoidable mishap, one moment in full enjoyment of life, the next moment fully dead
> Men and women in their prime, leaving children grieving for their parents
> Elderly people, not deserving such a vicious end to their long years.

Let us hold before God those who have been seriously injured on the roads whose lives will never be the same again, who may face years of pain, hardship and misery, dependent on others to supply their needs and to provide constant care.

Let us hold before God those who have been hurt in lesser ways, yet who still live out the terror and trauma of an incident that refuses to go away, whose confidence has been replaced by fear.

We remember before God those who are left behind, to rue the day when their loved ones were taken from them by sudden or long-drawn out death. Some may still hold a burning anger and sense of injustice where there is no one to take the blame, or at the very least to say sorry for their actions which might bring a degree of comfort to a broken heart.

We remember before God those who tend their injured and deprived loved ones, nursing them through long days and long nights, giving care and attention and dedication to an extent that may surprise even themselves.

Let us thank God for all who give comfort and consolation to the dying, the injured and the bereaved; for their family and friends who give support; for colleagues who give help in their work; and for strangers who come to their aid in times of emergency and sudden need.

Let us thank God, above all things, for the coming of Jesus Christ, the Word made flesh, Wisdom born as one of us, so that all who know Christ may know wisdom as she walks among us in this world. We thank God for his bridging the awful chasm between death and new life, which has restored to us the hope of life where life has no right to be.

God of light, cast away from us all the shadows and sorrows of our life on earth. Where your light seems to us faint and far off, sustain us in your love; where we see the new dawn of peace and justice, bring us to the clear light of day; and where your light shines bright for us in this life, bring us to the searing purity of your eternal life.

May God's care and love surround us; may God's promise re-unite us with all those we love; and may God's steadfast mercy bring us to a new heaven and a new earth. Through Jesus Christ our Lord.
Amen

RoadPeace
England

Prayer in Memory of Two Children Killed in a Road Tragedy

Cradle, O Lord, in your arms everlasting,
those who now suffer sore anguish and pain:
warmed may they be by true human affection;
by love surrounded in your care remain.

Cradle. O Lord, in your arms everlasting,
all who seek here for your comfort today;
make of our lives prayers of joyful self-giving,
offered to Christ who is light for the way.

Christopher Bradnock
RoadPeace
England

Eric

Eric, aged 20, son of Peter and Rosemary Raine, brother to Sarah and Vickie and uncle to Harley was killed at 11.20 pm on 4 June 2001 as a rear seat passenger.

Once a child who kept on growing
His song and laughter always flowing,
The constant doorbell, his telephone tone,
In this life he was never alone.

Try to remember his jokes, his schemes,
The clothes, his trainers, the cars, his gold,
He had it all except getting old.
Please don't let his death be in vain,
As that would add to our family's pain.

The Raine Family
England

Prayer of Intercession for Safety on Our Roads

We pray for all who work to promote greater safety on our roads:

> for highway surveyors and planners, construction and maintenance staff,
> Vehicle designers, safety researchers and technicians, and accident
> investigators;
> for those who promote and educate – road safety officers, school teachers,
> parents, crossing patrollers and motoring, cycling and pedestrian
> organisations;
> for those in parliaments and councils, who legislate and resolve on our behalf
> for greater safety and for lobbying groups who seek justice and fairness

We pray for those who deal with the effects of collisions and crashes:

> for the emergency services who attend, the police, ambulance staff and fire
> officers;
> for those who treat the injured victims, paramedics, doctors, nurses,
> surgeons and hospital staff.

We give thanks for their awareness of the sanctity and preciousness of every
human life; make them aware, Lord God, of our gratitude.

RoadPeace
England

Let Us Reach Beyond the Winter

*(written for people who suffer from Seasonal Affective Disorder (SAD) or who
simply long for brighter days – literally or metaphorically).*

Let us reach beyond the winter
through this dark, depressive gloom,
may the light of Christ come shining
into every shuttered room.

May the sunshine of the springtime
warm each frozen heart and mind,
melting prejudice and anger
by love faithful, strong and kind.

Now profound anticipation
wakens hope and offers grace,
as we press, with God beside us,
to the future we must face.

God who shares our darkest moments,
God of harmony and praise,
lead us on until you greet us,
God the goal of all our days.

Andrew Pratt
England

Cancer

You are the illness we dare not name,
like some swearword or evil incantation.
You are the monster beneath the bed,
the bogeyman who haunts the house.
You are the bully prowling in the playground,
scavenger hunting with the pack,
preying on the isolated, weak and vulnerable.
Yes, you can intimidate, hurt, disfigure and kill,
but, finally, you are a figment, a fraud.
For all your posturing, where is your power?
You cannot stifle my faith or extinguish my love.
You cannot break the bonds between family and friends.
You cannot erase my memories or erode my hope.
You cannot reach my spirit or breach my soul.
You cannot daunt my determination or buckle my courage.
You cannot assault my assurance or disturb my peace.
And come between me and my God?
I would laugh if I wouldn't cough blood!
You can destroy me but you can never defeat me.
So do your worst, give me your best shot:
for my murder is your suicide,
and your judgement, my glory.

Kim Fabricius
Wales/USA

The Good Samaritan

Hug me,
Pray for me,
Sit with me in the stillness please.

I have a grief as deep as oceans
And a need as high as mountains.
So hold my hand,
Hug me,
Sit quietly by my side,
But I beg of you
Do not
Do not weep for me.

For you see only
Grief
Echoing from my heart,
Oceans of pain reflected in my eyes.
And you are right.
Your eyes do not deceive you.
But come
And stand in my shoes.

If you could look through my eyes
Then what privilege it would be
To know
The joy of being
The stranger who is loved,
Unconditionally loved,
To feel the warmth of your compassion,
Drink in the fragrance of your tender prayers.

If you could see
Through my eyes
You would see beyond the pain,
Beyond the mist of tears,
To glorious glimpses of amazing love,
The healing and eternal love of God,
And know
That you were meeting face to face
The Good Samaritan
On the dusty road.

So hug me,
Pray for me,
Sit with me in the stillness please
But do not
Do not weep for me.

Pat Marsh
England

Living and Dying with HIV/AIDS

Charles:

In 1983 he became one of the first people in this country (England) to be diagnosed with AIDS. He hid his homosexuality from his macho work colleagues where jokes about 'poofters' were common. There was little support in those days, he had no close friends or counselling and lived with his mother who was still hoping he would 'find a nice girl'. In despair he committed suicide. Rumours of his HIV status leaked out; his workmates panicked and his mother received hate mail.

Our Prayer:

Give us compassion even when we do not understand. Let us not fear the unknown but let God turn our fear into courage so that we can comfort those in need and give them strength.

Andrew:

He is still a very successful businessman. When very young Andrew was on a business trip to Thailand and went with a prostitute. He had a glandular fever-like illness when he returned but soon felt well and thought no more about it. Eventually Andrew found the girl he wanted to marry and decided to have a thorough health check before proposing. He was found to be HIV positive. Andrew did not know what to do and was overwhelmed by guilt and grief. On his way home he did what he had not done since early childhood - he went into church and prayed.

Our Prayer:

Give us the conviction that God's forgiveness is limitless. When we look at our own lives we are so aware of the actions and words that we want to undo. Help us to show God's love to those who are in times of great need.

Joshua:

He was a Ugandan refugee and was eventually joined in this country (England) by Mary his wife and Joyful, their six year old daughter. They settled well and Joyful loved her school. They were all delighted when Mary became pregnant again. Soon after their baby was born, Joshua developed pneumocystis pneumonia and a diagnosis of AIDS was made. Joyful was the only one who had escaped the infection. By the time she was eight years old she was the only one still alive.

Relatives in Uganda wanted to take Joyful back there but she had lost her father, mother and brother – she said her friends in this country were all she had left. Until the AIDS diagnosis they were regular church worshippers but then they felt ashamed and did not attend again. No one came to see what had happened.

Our Prayer:

> Help us to be more aware of others' needs and give us the grace to know the right words of comfort. May our churches care for all, whatever race, colour, ethnic grouping, patterns of worship or difference from ourselves.

Margaret:

After marring an American, Bruno, Margaret went to live in the USA. She did not know that he was bisexual and when he died of pneumonia there was a conspiracy of silence so that she did not know it was AIDS related. Margaret was left with two young sons and eventually returned to England. Three years later she met and a year later, married a childhood sweetheart. Then came a welcome pregnancy and another son was born. A visitor from the States accidentally let slip that Bruno had, in fact, had AIDS. Margaret was tested and was positive: her only joy was that the baby and her new husband were both fine. She learnt the amazing way of living – to accept whatever happens – and she plans for a future, not knowing if she will have one, and lives each day to the full. She is happy and serene with no bitterness.

Our Prayer:

> Help us to face up to whatever tragedies come our way, knowing that we are never alone. God shares both our joy and our sorrow, so we should also stand beside those in need of comfort and support.

> *United Reformed Church*
> *Church and Society*
> *United Kingdom*

Rosa, an HIV+ Mozambican

Rosa is 23 years old and one of two million HIV+ Mozambicans.

Rosa's husband, in denial, refuses to be tested. She says he's been her only sexual partner. He is in a chronic-TB ward. In Mozambique, tuberculosis is a common opportunistic HIV-related infection. Usually it is fatal. Rosa, statistically in Mozambique may live about six more years.

She will go to work for as long as she can. Clean, cook, launder, leave the place each day more orderly than she found it. She rests between tasks and paces herself. Her employers understand. Rosa spends all the time she can with her three-year-old son who shows no signs of HIV. She is going back to school at nights as she had almost finished high school when her baby arrived.
She's reading books and pamphlets on living with HIV. The prices of western pharmaceuticals put them beyond the reach of Mozambicans so she is learning others strategies to give the best life possible. Certain vitamins and proteins in local vegetables, less sugar and plenty of exercise plus her faith. Because of these things her condition has stabilised.
She takes long baths, wears stylish clothes, pays skilful attention to hairstyle. These things matter. When she looks good she feels better and she's saying to everyone who sees her: 'I am worth caring for. I am valued.'

Rosa's real name is not published as she can't speak publicly about her condition. That is a lot to ask of her, in a national culture of denial which is changing slowly. She's not a public, spectacular leader. She is a young woman doing her best with terrible conditions around and inside her.

A Church held a candlelight memorial service for all the people who had died of AIDS in Mozambique. At the close, people lit candles and planted them on the lawn after dark in the shape of a red loop of ribbon, symbol of the war against AIDS. A poster mounted in the chancel reads: ''The Church has HIV/AIDS.' When one part of the body is affected the whole body suffers' '' Following St Paul, if the church consists of its members united as one body, then everyone has HIV.

For Rosa and the millions like her, healing may not mean physical cure but it can mean confirmed love, affirmed individual human value and an end to stigma and isolation.

Karen and Bill Butt
Mozambique

O God, Put My Broken Pieces Together

I'm bitter and I know that only God can rid me of my bitterness.
I'm broken and I know that only God can put my broken pieces together
I'm disappointed with myself and I know that only God can assure me that there is healing beyond my disappointment.
I'm afraid to trust again but I know that God can be trusted and that God will enable me to trust even if somewhere along the line I may be disappointed again, hurt again.
I'm weak but I know that God will give me new strength.
I'm sad but I know that God will give me new joy.
I'm angry at others, at myself.
I'm afraid and I feel overwhelmed. I know that God will be my constant companion.

O God, be near me as always.
Be within me as always.
Be around me as always.
Be before me as always.
And let me hear you.
And let me see you.
And let me love you in the ones whom I've hurt.
In the ones whom I've disappointed,
In the ones who I have made sad as well as in the ones who have hurt me,
In the ones who have disappointed me,
In the ones who have made me sad.
Let me see myself in you and you in me.

O God, come now in Jesus.
Come now in the Spirit.
Take hold of me.
Amen

Romero L del Rosario
The Philippines

Being There

In the deepest depths of pain
Of tiredness
Of vulnerability and fear;

I need you.

I do not need your words
Or wise advice

I just need you.

You and me together
In the stillness.
Holding my hand as I weep,
Cradling me in the warmth of your love.

In the silence
Together.

Easing the loneliness,
Sharing the pain.
Just being beside me
In your unknowingness.
Knowing that you cannot know the details
Of my tortured mind,
Can never plumb these depths of pain.

The comfort of your presence
Brings healing.

Your hand on mine.
Your thoughts
So closely intertwined with mine
In a deep embrace
Of love,
A deep acknowledgement of my needs …

That I need you

Just

To be there.

Pat Marsh
England

Resourceful and Resilient

St Mary's – A Life-giving Source

'My name is Suhana. I do embroidery work in St Mary's. We are a family of seven, including my parents and five children. We are three sisters and two brothers. My father is a rickshaw driver and my mother is a housewife. Whenever she gets free time she helps me with the embroidery work, my sister helps too. One of my brothers is learning to be a motor mechanic and the other one is doing tailoring.

'My sister and I got married on the same day. We had been doing embroidery to collect money for our wedding. After the wedding I was in my husband's house together with the in-laws. I became pregnant, but unfortunately the baby was dead in the womb before the delivery. I was operated on and the baby was removed. That was reason enough for my husband and in-laws to abandon me. My husband divorced me. So I went back to stay with my parents and do embroidery.

'Last year [2002] on 28th February, there was a break out of communal violence and everything that we owned was destroyed: our house and all the things that we had in the house. We stayed in a camp for several months.

'It was the generosity and concern of Sister Lucia that helped us to rebuild the house. Now we stay in our own houses again. What we went through was unforgettable. But St. Mary's has always been there to listen to our cry and to help us by providing the work of embroidery. Working in St. Mary's has helped us to earn our own personal expenses and also to help in the family to run the house.

'I can say that St Mary's has been and is a life-giving source to us. Without St Mary's we are incomplete. This institution is more beloved to us than our own life."

Background to St Mary's
In 1954, a group of Dominican nuns arrived in Ahmedabad, India, to start a hospital. Ahmedabad was an industrial city, producing textiles, but when the mills began to close many men lost their jobs and women became the sole earners. As a result, the nuns organized a sewing/embroidery centre, where women use traditional skills to make handicrafts.
The women at St Mary's also have access to medical help, saving schemes, cooking classes and scholarships for children.
Their beautiful embroidered products are sold by organisations like Traidcraft, which has been working with St Mary's for 21 years.

Traidcraft
England

The Master Furniture Maker

Kanyauju Nathan, who lives in south-west Uganda, is also known by his nickname 'Cameleon'. He moves by pulling himself along on the floor using his arms and two metal blocks. He is a master furniture maker. Kanyauju is married and he and his wife have six children. Other people help him in his workshop which is in a part of an old government building where he lives with other squatters. Cameleon is an example of someone who has overcome his disability and who is an inspiration with his well known sense of humour and his Christian faith which he expresses through songs which he writes and sings, accompanied on his guitar which he made himself. Unfortunately he was unable to stop thieves stealing his timber and so he needs to negotiate jobs with part payment in advance to buy new materials, He and his family live a day at a time. He needs help to keep him functioning as a small entrepreneur.

Ian Sanderson
England

An Interview with Anne Begg MP

Anne Begg has a rare genetic condition called Gaucher's Disease. One effect of this is to cause the bones in the legs to crumble slowly. Problems began when she was a teenager. This made life difficult for her but she has never given in. She became the first person in Scotland to teach from a wheelchair and now she has become the first wheelchair-using MP.

What was it like when you found out you were becoming disabled?

Anne: I had a very difficult time. I became very shy because of how I looked. I thought everybody was staring at me.

What did you do after you went to university?

Anne: I was a secondary school teacher for nineteen years. I absolutely adored teaching. I miss it a bit now but not things like marking.

I was told when I was seventeen that I couldn't be a teacher. But I did – not only did I become a teacher but I was promoted. No one can now say to anyone who is in a wheelchair that they cannot be a teacher because I've done it.

So how did you become an MP

Anne: I joined the Labour Party in 1983. When the Labour Party was looking for more women candidates, a number of people said that I should apply. They thought I could do the job. It was too good a chance to miss. I got elected in 1997 and it's the best thing I've ever done in my life.

What issues are you interested in?

Anne: MPs can't know about everything. I am very interested in education because I was a teacher. I'm also very much in favour of stem cell research.

How much have you personally suffered from prejudice or discrimination?

Anne: Almost daily, I face it every time I reach a building I can't get into. I face it from people who speak to the person who is with me and ignore me. People think you're invisible in a wheelchair. I get very angry with that. And the transport system in the country is a disgrace though it's getting better.

Could you give me a couple of examples?

Anne: Well, last year I used the London Underground for the first time! I can now get on most trains. Previously I was always put into the guard's van.

What does that feel like?

Anne: I cannot describe how small and humiliated it makes you feel. I have a great life and I do not regret the fact that I am disabled in any way but if I turn up somewhere and I can't get in then I feel I am being rejected.

I've always found in my life that if I want to do something there will be a way of achieving it. So it's not the disability, it's the person's ability that matters.

John Grooms
England

My Friend Marty

My friend Marty is clever when walking,
When he goes out his white stick is feeling –
Finding the steps and the kerbs and the pavements
All of the time he walks.

My friend Marty is clever at listening,
There at the zebra traffic is slowing,
When the bleep goes then he crosses in safety;
All the way home he knows.

My friend Marty is clever when reading –
Over the page his fingers go searching,
Over the small raised-up dots they are feeling
All of the time he reads.

My friend Marty is clever at telling
What's for a meal when dinner is cooking,
Who sucks a peppermint, who's got an orange –
So many things he knows!

My friend Marty is clever at strumming,
Over the strings his fingers are going;
Clear in his thinking his brain will be hearing
All of the tunes he'll play.

My friend Marty is clever at knowing
Each of our voices spoken in greeting:
'Hallo there Marty!' 'Oh, hallo there Jenny!'
Soon as he hears he knows.

Cecily Taylor
England

Invitation

Meet me in the garden
The wheelchair path
Defined routes scream directions
This way only no short cuts.

Large orange symbols
Keep me in my place
Control my moving
In this beautiful place.

Who will walk beside me?
Walk along the path
Stay within the boundaries
Join me on my journey.

Tell me your stories
Sister to sister
Where do we start
Breaking down the boundaries.

Jean Palmer
England

My Dream is to Learn Computer Skills

My name is Sonu and I am 21 years old. I live in Indira Puram with my parents, two sisters and two brothers. We live in a rented house. My elder sister is 23 years old and works in a factory. My younger sister is studying at secondary school. I have two younger brothers who are also at school.

My father is handicapped. Ten years ago he lost his eye in a truck accident, unfortunately medical treatment did not help. Thankfully, he still can see a little from his other eye, but he has no work now. Formerly he was a worker building houses. He could find work at that time at least for twenty days a month. But life was never easy and there was not enough money to meet the household needs. My mother remained a housewife, she is not in good health either. In spite of these difficulties we still managed to go to school.

Due to economic problems a few years ago my sister Seema had to leave school. She worked for one year in a factory to help the family. The factory does not pay enough and only gives jobs on a temporary basis. When my sister lost her job, I also had to leave the school. Now I am enrolled there as a private student. I was badly in need of a job. I went to find work in several factories but it was difficult. One day I came into contact with Madhu who had been working with Tara Projects. She advised me to visit the workshop and explain about my situation. I was heard sympathetically and got the work immediately. I felt welcomed there.

I have been working here for a year and am still learning. We are happy that Tara Projects gives us work. I know the project works to help women and pays fair wages. I am happy that I get more money now. It is a good environment here, so I like to work here. We like to be busy.

The good change is that I earn money now and I am able to help my sister and brothers go to school. I help to pay for their education. Every month I save money in my bank account. The rest of the money I give to my mother for the household expenses and to pay for school fees for my sister and brothers.

My dream is to learn computer skills and be able to help my sister and brothers to complete their education. Good education will certainly help our socio-economic standards.

We are thankful to Traidcraft, for giving us employment. We try our best to improve ourselves. We hope that the Tara Projects will continue to give us work.

Background on Tara Projects

Tara Projects is a non-profit organisation based in Delhi, serving some 25 community-based groups of artisans from all regions in North India.

They have been supplying Traidcraft for over 20 years andare currently Traidcraft's biggest supplier of crafts.

Tara's objective is to help craft workers to achieve self-sufficiency by providing income-generating opportunities and developing marketing skills. They have brought about major changes in these craft groups and their communities due to fair trade sales.

Traidcraft
England

Mature Women

The mature women of today
are determined to strive
for what is good,
and to better their lives.
Some go to college
and some to night school
with faith, determination
to reach their goal.
Some husbands think
wives are wasting their time,
but to women, the things they are doing
suits them fine.
Most of the women
have gained great knowledge
by going back to school
and to college.
These ambitious women
know what they want,
they go out and get it,
They are doing no harm.
Some are grandmothers
that is no problem,
one day their studying
will all be behind them.
So don't laugh and sniff
at the things that we do
why not come and join us
and be a mature student too.

Myrtle Walker
Jamaica/England

The Smile Is Something Special

Some children make a lasting impression. There is something they say, or something they do, or something they wear, that stays with you. If you meet them again as adults you still see the memorable child in the perhaps unremarkable adult. With her, it wasn't saying or doing – since she couldn't say anything and there wasn't a great deal that she could do. But she had a smile like dawn breaking over the hills. One of those smiles that made you feel good, however you had felt before. You came to do good for a little girl in a long-stay hospital ward and you went away having been done good to.

With severely disabled children, there are smiles which seem to have everything to do with their internal world and nothing to do with the world and people around them. Her smiles were of a different kind. They were about appreciation of people and responding to people and they drew people to her. Sometimes, although we all assumed that she could not understand verbal jokes the smile became a giggle and it seemed that the joke had been understood.

She did not have a great deal to smile about. Her back was bent in two different directions. Her legs didn't work at least not in any conventional way – sometimes they jerked. There was a little grip in one hand but otherwise her upper limbs didn't do what they were meant to do either. She lay in one position or another, usually looking rather uncomfortable – light enough to lift but not easy to lift because her back didn't bend. I held her while her bed was changed after her bath: a smile at one end and two little cold feet at the other end. It struck me that she had probably never seen her feet.

I met her again thirty years on, still lying in that uncomfortable shape. At one end the feet emerged below the covers, At the other end, the smile – still a very special smile – greeting me across the room. Again, I was glad I had come.

Mencap
England

GCSEs Don't Come Into It

A small group of parents were celebrating GCSE results. The star was a girl who had secured a well deserved six As and five Bs. The conversation moved on to the value or otherwise of AS levels and university prospects. The conversation tailed away when Mrs Brown joined the group. She asked how all the young people had done and the conversation was re-run in a more subdued – indeed almost apologetic way.

Eventually, someone had to ask Mrs Brown, 'How is Anthony getting on?' Anthony is the same age as the other young people, but he has severe learning difficulties, severe epilepsy and autism. He goes to a residential school where his needs and behaviour are better addressed. Mrs Brown smiled happily

'We thought we had lost him last week after the third fit in one morning; but we spoke to the staff later in the day and could hear him singing away in the background. They said that he was having a really good day and had eaten the best part of three lunches.' Seeing the looks on her neighbours' faces she said 'It's alright you get a different view of things when you have a severely impaired child with a life-threatening condition. Being alive; being happy and recognising you with a hug, means everything. Homework and GCSEs don't come into it.'

Mencap
England

Taking A Chance

Jamie McCoy is a former homeless person and Crisis Changing Lives aware recipient. Recently, Jamie reeived the Student of the Year prize form London's City Literary College after completing an extraordinary turnaround after thirty years of homelessness and addiction. Just three years ago, Jamie, now 52, was close to despair. His visit to a Crisis Open Christmas shelter helped convince him to change his life and to keep his mind busy, he taught himself to read and write. Now Jamie is renowned for his moving poetry and has gained a qualification in computing too. Crisis Changing Lives helped him pay course fees and buy a word processor with email to keep in touch with supportive new friends, reinforcing Jamie's determination to leave homelessness behind for good.

Stepping Stones, issue number five 2003 (the journal of Crisis)

Bowl of cornflakes cup of tea
Newspaper upon my knee
My two best friends and someone new
What would they say if they knew?
I look at papers pictures fine
Words are just a squiggly line
Feeling low and really old
This is the secret that I hold

Bluffed my whole life through
Always thought I was stupid too
I'd put together pictures and old news
Sometimes I'd get so confused
How do I say I can't write or read?
But inside I have this growing need
I want to read just like you
So I can have a point of view

Now to take the step the hardest part
Learn A B C from the start
Hard as it may seem
Just take a chance and live your dream

Jamie McCoy
Via Crisis Changing Lives
England

Living on the Edge of Communities

Lord, we pray for those living on the edge of communities:

For women trapped in violent relationships, afraid to leave
because they have nowhere safe to take their children,
living each day in fear, making the kids keep quiet in case they get hit;
Help us to love one another as you love us.

For asylum seekers, often running for their lives and risking everything,
yet now facing suspicion, forced to move from place to place,
unable to get work or claim benefits;
Help us to love one another as you love us

For young people leaving care, alone and unsupported
without the safety net of a family,
fending for themselves on the streets;
Help us to love one another as you love us

For those who sleep on the pavement tonight
because all the hostels are full;
Help us to love one another as you love us

May we grow in love and faithfulness
as we build your new community on earth.

Rachel Lampard and Jennie Richmond
England

Undervalued - All in a Day's Work

He worked hard all day.
Dry-stone walling.
That night he suffered a stroke
Aged 78
Working days now over.

Time to reflect,
How people viewed his work.
A skilled craft.
Must be preserved.
People pay to learn.
For him
It was just another task.
All in a day's work
For a farm labourer.

I remember frosty February,
Hedge-laying, layering,
Taming the tangled blackthorn,
Billhook razor sharp,
Leather gloves scant protection.
At night he probed with a needle,
Unflinchingly removing the thorns.
Dabbed each spot with iodine.
A skill, a craft.
All in a day's work
For a farm labourer.

In pre-combine days,
Grain was stacked in a rickyard
Awaiting the threshing machine,
Thatched with wheat straw,
Watertight against the weather.
His thatcher's tools were simple,
Knee-pads cut from old car tyres
A comb made with six inch nails
Ancient sheep shears.
He took a special pride in this task.
A skill, a craft,
All in a day's work
For a farm labourer.

These rustic crafts
Sound quaint
In a computerised age.
Yet these skills
Which had to be learnt
Passed down
Nurtured by some rural mentor
Drawing on human versatility.
Society could only see a farm labourer.
That's what he was paid to be.
In reality
He was a multi-skilled Rural Operative.

Y Mochyn Daear
England

The Rocky Road

Virupakshi is a young boy who lives near a remote rural town in the drought prone part of northern Karnataka State, south India. His left leg was paralysed at the age of three as a result of polio. He was luckier than many children in the area because an India Non-Governmental Organisation (NGO) had a clinic near his home town of Deodurg. His mother was taught basic physiotherapy exercises at the clinic to help release the contractures in his leg. Once this was done his family bought him a caliper made at the NGO workshop. This enabled him to walk independently.

Virupakshi's next problem was getting to school since the road from his house was very rocky. Undeterred, his mother got together with the local community to remove the rocks and make the road safe for her son.

Virupakshi's ambition is to be a doctor.

Ruth Patil
south India/England

A Useful Member of Her Community

The best time for Mudamma, a young woman who is married with a young baby, is festival time. She is able to earn extra money for her family as a result of her sewing skills. Mudamma was twelve when she came into contact with the Indian NGO (see above). She was living with polio but over the course of seven years she benefited greatly from advice, support, surgery, physiotherapy and later a vocational training course. As a result she was equipped with tailoring skills which are very useful in her remote village community. Mudamma lives one kilometre from the centre of the village and it is not easy for her to trek across the barren, rocky terrain to meet the villagers. She often has to look after her baby by herself. When the rains fail and the crops do not grow her husband has to migrate to towns or cities to earn money. Sometimes there is no work so it is important for Mudamma to use her skills to make saris.

Geoffrey Duncan
south India/England

Ordinary People: Ordinary Moments

In October 2003 when Devamma, a 14 year-old girl from a remote village in Raichur District, North Karnataka, south India read about the President of India accepting the credentials of the new British High Commissioner to India she was very surprised.   She did not know the High Commissioner when he was Designate but she did know Michael Arthur, the man behind the designation. Devamma and her family were his hosts for two days when Mr Arthur stayed with them as part of a community immersion process that was organised by Plan International and the India Office of the Department for International Development of the Government of the United Kingdom.

Devamma and Michael have very little in common except the desire to be involved with the world around them.

Devamma lost the partial use of her left leg to bone tuberculosis (TB) at the age of 7 years. Initially, her parents did not understand why she kept saying her leg was getting weaker. It was only when her left knee got locked and she was forced to hobble around that her parents took her to a Samarthya Disability Assessment Clinic *. Staff referred her to an orthopaedic surgeon at the Raichur Town government hospital. After a series of tests she was diagnosed as having bone TB. She was put on the appropriate medication. It took eighteen months for her leg to heal. During that time the TB led to her left leg becoming shorter. While the Samarthya orthotics workshop was able to prepare a knee brace and a customised sandal with a raised sole this period was not easy for a girl who had always been very active.

A knee operation was carried out at the Sindhi Charitable hospital in Bangalore. As a result she has partial movement in the knee. Devamma has not let her disability affect her interests. She insisted on continuing with school after completing Class 5. The nearest middle school was 5 kilometres away and most people thought she was doubly handicapped because of her gender and her locomotor limitations. Now Devamma who studies in Class 7 walks to school and back from her village every day. When she is in her village she is busy volunteering with the local health group to popularise immunisation and participating in the meetings of Prati Dwani which is the local Organisation of People with Disabilities.

Michael Arthur was previously the Director-General for European Union and Economics in the UK government. While he had been involved with Indian affairs for a long time he decided that he would better understand the country and the people if he was able to experience and share their lives without the intrusion of the pomp and paraphernalia that would surround him in his new appointment as High Commissioner. When papers were sent to him about the community immersion process Michael was curious. Community Immersion was devised as an opportunity for people whose decisions affect the lives of the poor to meet some of the people who are most affected by their decisions. Also, he read about the different development organisations, who partner the work of Plan International in India and who had agreed to host community immersion participants. Michael chose to visit SAMUHA ** because he was curious about this organisation which is involved in village development, community based rehabilitation of people with disabilities, HIV/AIDS, watershed development and other aspects of development.

SAMUHA staff spoke to Devamma and her father about a foreigner who wanted to get to know more about people. They were both amused that someone should find their ordinariness of interest and curious as to who would want to experience a life they were trying to get away from. Also, they were worried: how do you prepare for a guest you don't know anything about?

B Hampanna, assistant director of Samarthya, the SAMUHA disability sector met Michael at Raichur railway station and was his local friend and translator along with Suresh Kushtagi, a SAMUHA staff member, who is disabled, at 01.30 to meet the train from Bangalore. They stayed with Michael until he left Raichur four days later by road for Hyderabad.

'Michael didn't just immerse himself in our lives and our work. His interest in everything around him was so complete that it forced you out of yourself and made you look at things differently.
He said, contradictorily, 'I am exhausted and I am renewed'.

He should have been exhausted. He saw how a smokeless wood burning stove prevented tearful, red eyes; how a stone slab floor in houses whose floors had not been raised, prevented rain water from seeping in and prevented the young and the old from becoming ill by sleeping on the ground in damp sheets; how a small investment in plastering a mud mortar wall prevented rains from eroding it and how this lengthened the life of the house and prevented the family from sliding further into poverty because of their inability to invest in a new house; how a nala (natural drain) helped to reduce the velocity of rain water and contributed to recharging the water table; how people with disabilities took pride in accessing rural housing schemes as a right and without making any informal payments; that rural women, the elderly, and the young in rural communities were beginning to talk about HIV/AIDS and how they needed to mobilise themselves to deal with the after effects of this; how village men had become teachers and were able to deliver quality education in hamlets without access to public transportation or to government schools.

Devamma's father put the visit in a different perspective. 'We were worried whether he would eat our food, or whether he would be comfortable staying with us. The first night we made a special bed for him on a charpoy (stringed cot) and we all went to sleep on the roof of our house. We were surprised when he joined us on the roof and slept on the ground like all of us. When you wake up and see someone sleeping like you, you realise they are not different from you.'

Ordinary moments. When you realise you are no different from anyone else around you.

T Pradeep
south India

* Samarthya
Samarthya is the disability sector of SAMUHA. The word is from the Kannada language spoken in Karnataka State. It means 'potential' and expresses a philosophical belief that guides all of Samarthya's work: that the key determinant of a person's value is their potential, not their disabilities or impairments.

** SAMUHA
SAMUHA is an Indian non-governmental organisation which is involved in village development, community-based rehabilitation of people with disabilities and impairments, in HIV/AIDS, watershed development and the empowerment of women.

A Litany for Understanding and Infinite Love

I was motivated to write this litany after reading the piece by T Pradeep about Michael Arthur. With people like Michael Arthur as High Commissioner for India I believe there is another sign of hope for the world. I have been actively involved with SAMUHA/Samarthya for some years and the other departments mentioned in the above description. There is a tremendous need for education, understanding and active prayer to be put into practice, not only for the plight of marginalised people in India but for all people in similar circumstances whether the country is so-called developed or developing.

God of the Infinite in Caring Love enable us to be very uncomfortable because of:

The indifference of the masses to the need for clean water;
   for the many times when water is wasted on a daily basis;
   for the apparent inconvenience when pipes are laid for even better water supply;
   for the times when we cry out for rain and then complain when it comes.

The indifference of the masses to the problems of physical impairments,
   for the impatience which grows toward the person in a wheelchair;
   for the ignorance caused by lack of knowledge and not wanting to know;
   for the fear of encountering someone who needs our help.

The indifference of the masses to the plight of people who have no access to better health,
   for the times when we turn to drugs as a crutch for a minor ailment;
   for the way in which we indulge in private health care when the NHS fails to meet our needs;
   for the disregard we have for the failing health of millions of people around the world.

The indifference of the masses to the basic needs of the hungry,
   for the lack of a balanced diet to enable all humankind to take part in healthy living;
   for the indulgence of the directors and executive staff at the company dinner;
   for the times when we forsake the idea of a frugal lunch in case it offends some people.

The indifference of the masses to the need for sustainable development in rural communities,
   for the worry caused to the people in drought prone areas of the world;
   for the suicide rate amongst farmers who lose their livelihoods in many countries;
   for the women who struggle to create handicrafts for income and keep their families alive.

God of the Infinite in Caring Love

Give us the will to tackle the problem of polluted water;
to ensure that clean water
comes high on the budgets of national governments
before bombs and lethal weapons of destruction.

Give us the will to explore ways
to eradicate life destroying illnesses
so that healthy living for everyone around the globe
is a way of life.

Give us the will to remove poverty from around the globe;
to ensure that financial institutions,
world organisations and national governments
raise their targets so that
talk becomes reality and no longer myth.

God of Infinite love,
In your tender care,
Strengthen us as your agents,
Your prayer activators,
To make our acts of faith
Deeds of compassion
In the knowledge that our dedication,
Motivated by your love,
Christ's compassion,
and the creative impulses of the Holy Spirit
Will bring hope and life to your world.

Amen

Geoffrey Duncan
south India/England

One Day at Emmaus

Kevin found, at Emmaus, a way back from homelessness and drug addiction, a pit he fell into after a broken marriage. The man most would have classed as a 'layabout' became the Community book-keeper and a trusted Companion, a listener whom others turned to if they had a problem.

> Karen ended up in prison at 19, a rebel determined to affront her mother with parties, drink, drugs, boys. Released, she came to Emmaus, where she has rebuilt a life and become reconciled with her mother.

Richard's high pressure financial sector job pushed him over the edge, into drink and onto the streets. At Emmaus, he rediscovered long-forgotten wood working skills he learnt from his grandfather. 'You learn humility and tolerance,' he says. 'In return you gain confidence, trust and real friendship.'

> A three-year-old shouldn't watch his father beat his mother, but Stephen did. After fifteen years on the streets of London, wandering, looking for the love he had lost as a child, he discovered Emmaus and shelter, dignity, security and purpose.

Every day people like these take another step towards rebuilding their lives. Every day, people like these live a life that is fulfilling, a life of dignity and self-respect and of value to those around them.

Every day others languish on the streets in need of the chance, the trust and the challenge that is Emmaus.

These people are Companions of Emmaus. Their names have been changed to protect their identity.

Emmaus UK
Cambridge England

God of the Emmaus Road

God of the Emmaus road
prompt us to see Christ
in the variety of people
we meet each day.

God of the Emmaus road
there they are ... the Big Issue seller
the homeless woman/man slumped in the shop doorway
the drug dependent person sitting alone,
pale and covered in a grotty old blanket ...
'spare any change'?

God of the Emmaus road,
help us to see the fear
the desperation
the potential
the honesty
in the eyes of the refugee and asylum seeker.

God of the Emmaus road,
keep us alert,
aware,
as to where the needs are

and then as we try to get to grips with life,
all around us,
grant us graciousness
love
patience

even when it is running out after a hard day
(what about others who have had it very tough)

God of the Emmaus road
make it possible for us to serve,
increasingly so,
as we stand up
and are counted
because we own up to our belief in the Compassionate Christ

Geoffrey Duncan
England

A Sri Lankan Journey

(January-March 2003)

Diane D'Souza travelled across the war-torn part of northern Sri Lanka after hostilities had ceased. These are her reflections of the experiences gained from the journey.

Heading North on the A9 I didn't realise the fragility
Of this paved Island track
The contested spine of your land.
I hadn't realised how new it was
To travel to the North
How people still marvelled at the
        Miracle of it
Being able to get to Jaffna
Inaccessible Jaffna
After so many years.

(Of course, travelling in the
Other Direction
Is a different problem
For those living in the
Beleaguered North
More stumbling
More fractured a journey
More questions
More visibility
More extortion
Making their way through
Check-post after check-post.
But that is another story
Another Journey.
Not mine.)

Head Count

I see cows unherded
Finding their way through forests and fields
Free to wander, unfettered convicts
A large complacent cud-chewing band
Lazing, nurturing young
Soaking up the soft early morning sun.
And I wonder, how many cows
Have been crippled by the mines?
And does any one count?

The First Taste

I remember waking at the crossroads
My travel-induced coma dissolving
At the sight of shops
Burned out and blackened
Their roofs caved in.
The bus quieted, time narrowed
As we drew a collective breath
Straining to see what was for many
Our first direct glimpse of it.
Touching—even if only with our eyes—
The terrifying face of war
The cold picked-over bones of it
The stirring incredulous grief of it
The sheer enormity
Of violence, loss, and hatred
Enshrined in these crumbling stones.

Along the Road

I wonder about death lurking in the fields
The barbed wire close to the road
The red signs with their threatening reminder
Of the bones beneath our flesh.
The sign boards hold cartoon depictions
Of careless men and women losing a leg
In graphic bloody explosions of earth.
"Beware of explosives"
"Your protection will save your limbs and life"
"Danger: beware of mines"
"Please avoid using both sides of the road"
"Your precaution ensures safety"
I miss my children.
I miss seeing children.
I miss the tickle of innocent laughter.
Instead I drink in
The sky and the Earth
The weight-less birds
Soaring over fields of wild grass
The complacent cows
Straying in from the jungle.

An Ode

I didn't notice you
Didn't really see you
At least not at first..

Is it any wonder?
So much was new
The fields wildly flowering.
The shells of homes
Like unkempt gravestones.
The signs blood red with
Skulls and crossed bones
Warning in a language
More universal than
Sinhala or English or Tamil:
Stick to the road
We give no guarantees
Make no promises
Assume no responsibility
For casual whims
Which take you
Into beckoning fields.
Never mind the cattle now wild
The peacocks with swaying unfurled tails
The grasses flowering into seed.
Stick to the road
Away from risk
Away from danger
Away from buried metal
Designed to maim.

Is it any wonder I missed you?
Missed your dignified presence
In this shouting silence
This too loud echo
Of gunfire recently stilled.
Your very stature
Your voiceless acceptance
Made you easy to overlook.
Your crippled scarred limbs
Silent as a shroud.

When I finally saw you
Really saw you
I was jolted awake
Questions tumbling
Suddenly into light:

Did the bullets hurt?
Did the shells lodged
Within your flesh
Cripple? Did they maim?
Or did you simply receive them
With a thud, a shake and a shudder
A terrified bird suddenly soaring up
Fleeing nest and young
With a frightened cry.

How many bullets, I wondered,
Does it take to kill a tree?

When I finally saw you
Realised just what I was seeing
Not knot-holes
Not casual scars…
My breath quickened
My lips parted incredulous
I scrambled for my camera
Needing to record, to remind
To enshrine the story told so
Wordlessly in your flesh
Tree after tree
Kilometre after kilometre
Heartbeat after heartbeat.

Oh my tree of many woundings
How could I have overlooked
The gaping holes which pepper your flesh
The protective lips sealing shattered bark
Hiding bullets lodged within you.
Your spreading canopy borne by
Limbs deformed—some dead and lifeless
Others pulsing with vivid green life.

Oh my tree of many woundings
How many souls took shelter
Hiding beneath your comforting branches
In fear or anger or boredom?
How many sought your refuge
Panting, heart thumping, shielded behind you?
How many left their blood mingling with sap
As their bodies received one last caress
Sliding down, returning to the Mother
Life draining into the very soil
From which you draw sustenance.

Oh my tree of many woundings
Rooted, generations old
Did you ever wonder
Or ponder
Or ache?
Did you die a little with each
Bite into your flesh
With each battle raging about you
Land won, land lost, land taken again
Holding within your fractured woody core
The bullets, the shells, the shrapnel
Those unwanted children of the
Careful union of gun powder and metal
Splintered badges of truth
For those who wish to see.

Oh my dear trees of the A9
I haven't even begun to learn
How many bullets a tree can bear
Its heart whole, its spirit intact
Its branches sheltering birds
Its creviced bark an invitation to
Scolding squirrels blessed with stripes
Its tender leaves and strips of bark
A gift to ghosts of goats who cluster
Gratefully beneath its spreading shadow.

Oh my rooted sisters of the A9
I long to caress your scarred flesh
To examine in minute loving detail
Your injuries, your healing
To place my fingers in knotted holes
To feel the swell of protective flesh
Marshalled to preserve, to transform.
You bear your wounds with dignity
Remembering, not forgetting
Your life guided by growth
By survival, by healing—
Drawing sustenance from the sun
Soaking up the blessing of rain
Living, pulsing, one more season.

Unexpected Respite

I was not prepared
For your wild beauty
I didn't know this face of war:
Nature reclaiming her own
The coveted, cosseted, abused land
Exploding, expanding
Celebrating the homecoming
Of Earth returning to her self.

Field and forest mingle now
In messy vibrant growth.
Except for those pock-marked avenues
Where soldiers ignited your fields
Vanquishing forests and tall grasses
Unassuming trees and bushes
Serving no purpose
Except to nurture life
Or provide persistent, resilient shelter
To those we fear.

At first I didn't notice
Didn't find remarkable
Your untrammelled beauty.
Then I saw the burnt-out homes
The warning signs, skulls on blood red,
And realised that cultivation, habitation
Are fallow words in fields pregnant
With gunfire and mines.

Now you and your creatures are
Alone to work, to live, to celebrate.
The peacocks spreading their tails
Dancing on buried explosives
Prancing on delicate machinery
Hidden in your rich dark womb.
They prove their comeliness
Before indifferent hens—
Such a profusion of birds, everywhere
I never realised that war brings this too:
Healing from restless relentless development.

War as respite.

Losing Clarity

Tell me again. Explain to me again the Cause
For as I walk this road it is getting harder and harder to see
Harder to hold onto the vision of The Great Freedom
The Great Struggle
The Great Injustice
The Great Liberation.
If I hold one more motherless child
If I see one more home destroyed
If I see one more child holding a gun
If I hear one more story of everything lost
If I see one more shrapnel-scarred tree
If I hold the hand of one more mother still searching for her child
If I wipe away one more tear of a child whose father won't come home
If I hear one more wistful remembrance of the time before
If I pass one more grave
If I see one more empty kilometre without a child
If I hear one more horrific statistic of loss
If I see one more kilometre of razor wire
If I learn one more fact about just how undernourished the children are
(the surviving ones)
I think I will burst
Cracking open like an overripe pomegranate
The seeds turned brown, no longer sweet
The ants devouring what remains of the juice.

Tell me again. Explain to me again the Cause
Because it is getting harder and harder to see
Harder to hold onto the vision of The Great Freedom
The Great Struggle
The Great Injustice
The Great Liberation.

Pulling Onions

I promised myself that I'll cry later
I, who am not afraid of tears,
Who honours the connection they bring
Who knows the importance of
Bridging emotion and intellect
As we wade through tragedy
As we walk blood-soaked ground.

Even knowing all this
I choose to weep later—
Right now there are
Too many threads to hold together
Too much work to get done.
I remember the women
Who used to hold tea parties
Visiting neighbours, making sweets
Who now pull onions from dry fields
For fifty rupees a day
While men plan the Big Job
The ultimate saving step
The work imbued with sufficient dignity
And the children wait with crying bellies.

We have more patience, they told us
Explaining why men aren't in the fields
We do it because it is necessary
We've learned to do it
We need the money
Besides, if you just give up
Falling down weeping
Over all you've lost
Over every child washed overboard
Over every cow and goat and chicken that was ours
Over land and village and a place called home
Then how would the children get fed
And go to school
And have a life
With more hope than ours?

And so, remembering my sisters,
I put down my head and pull onions
And I promise myself—
Biting my lips
Tasting the blood
Rubbing mud-smeared knuckles
Across my eyes—
That I will cry
Later.

For Visaka

I liked your boldness
The measure of your words
Knowing when to hold back
When to make a point strongly and well.
You wear your leadership
Like your sari: elegantly draped
With dignity and beauty.

I wonder how I could have forgotten
That we're in a land
Where not only mines are
Hidden below the surface.

How could I have neglected to see
That on this small island
When losses are counted
In tens of thousands
Even a gathering of twenty or thirty
Has the wounded right among us.
The ties are intimate and deep
To those who left too soon—
They're not statistics
But the faces of our own beloveds.
We feel not the pain of distant sisters,
But the cut of shrapnel
Lodged deep within our chests
Concealed behind smiling lips and
Articulate, thoughtful conversation.

I remember your son, Visaka,
The one still missing.
And the other one, too,
Still alive in the army.

My brave sister, I still carry within
The imprint of your passion
Your strength, your determination
Uniting women whose children are
Disappeared.
Struggling to bring
An end to This
Knowing the taste of loss
Knowing the wounding
Of not having even a grave
At which to offer flowers.
You bear your scars
With direct, clear eyes
The tears now glittering diamonds
Capturing and reflecting the light.

The Echoes

We have learned to distrust promises of time
So we board the bus prepared for anything
A ride of three hours could take ten.
The morning is young and soon we are
Immersed in the beauty of this island paradise.

The road to Batticoloa is smooth
Just as they said at the hotel.
Except, of course, for the detours around
The army encampments.
Our bus bumps over dirt tracks
As we skirt the barbed wire
Passing former check-posts with
Curious, casual boys in uniform
Standing around, killing time.
The oasis of trees and the distant walls
Screening all else from view.

When we pass the third camp
I turn to Leela to share a thought
Breaking our silent reverie.
But her eyes, I discover,
Have seen different ghosts from mine.
The third camp was the worst, she tells me,
They took prisoners there to be tortured.
You see how isolated it is,
So few people passing this way.
They say you could hear the screams
From quite a distance.

We both fall silent
As the bus lurches onto pavement
I crane my neck, watching
The oasis melt into the horizon
And I hear the piercing echoes
Of men delirious with pain
Beyond dignity, beyond humanity
Screaming for an end to this,
Any end—for God's sake
Crying for mercy, for release
Just make it stop
Please, make it stop.

I see isolated beauty differently now.

Pausing

I aim the camera
Bringing the collapsed roof
The burnt-out walls
Into focus.
Using the zoom,
Timing the shot to match
The bouncing of the bus,
Adjusting the composition
To capture the pulsing green
Springing to life
Amidst these deserted ruins.

But my heart is heavy
And I lower the camera
Realising that I cannot take
One more picture
Of devastation, of destruction.
Even if here it was
Freedom-seeking rebels not
Government-supported troops
Who led the massacre.

A desecrated home, a perished dream
Looks very much the same
Whoever throws the bomb.

Is It Worth It?

Remind me why I'm doing this.
Remind me why I have decided that
I need to do things differently.
Why I can't go on with things as they were.
Why I began this freedom struggle
Fighting for my soul
Wrestling for my survival
Resisting the path pulling me
Further and further from my self.
Rewriting my destiny.
Remind me why I'm here
Because hearing the pain-filled voices
Feeling the heaviness of my steps
Seeing the woundings fresh and bloody
Glimpsing the distance growing between us
I need to recall, to revisit

The Struggle
    The Hope
        The Promise
            The Liberation.
For all I see right now is the pain.

A Child's Reminder

We introduced ourselves
All of us, strangers and friends,
Right around the chaotic pulsing circle
Old, young, residents, guests
Displaced and those who still have a home.

It's been twelve years since they left
Forced to abandon land and home
In storm-tossed boats
Fleeing for their lives
Reaching an uncertain shore
Dazed by shock, by loss
By the violence of the leaving.

Twelve years later
Home is still that village left behind
Again and again I hear the
Sanctifying name of Mannar
A mantra of remembrance
A hymn of longing.

Until one bold child
Not knowing her place
Blurts out with twinkling eyes
The name of another home.
Mischievous girl
Reminding those who hear
That roots grow into this
Sand-packed earth of Puttalam
As in any other place—
Deep and sure.

Diane D'Souza
England/India/Sri Lanka

Reflections on Memories and Bereavement

To Ashley

To the young girl I never knew,
To the daughter I never met
Except in a busy hospital ward – dead.
I miss you.
I miss your smiles, I miss your tears,
I miss your laughter, hopes and fears,
And how you would have grown over the years.
Oh, how I miss you!
I miss your first words, your first breath, your first cry
Like the first green ash shoot reaching for the sky.
I miss potty training and helping you read
As the sapling grows and matures from the seed.
I miss watching your hair dancing in the breeze
Like a gentle wind rustling the thin ash leaves.
I miss boyfriends, your wedding, even the ring
As the ash tree buds and flowers in the spring.
I miss huddling you close out of the rain;
In a storm the broad ash boughs do much the same.
How much I love and miss you, now you'll never know,
Until I, too, die and into Christ's arms go.
Until we meet there and pain and death depart
I store my love for you deep inside my heart.
In His safe embrace our lives at last we'll share,
Until then, farewell, I leave you in His care.

Kevin Paul Woodbridge
England

Symbols

That Friday afternoon, crawling through fields of wood violets,
The stopping train from Tonbridge pulled into the station. It was empty.
Summer was at its hottest. He stared bleakly, trying to recall
What had been said.

The train crept forward. From the window he watched an elderly man
in his herb garden, tying together bunches of parsley and dill.
Hawthorn crowded the lanes. He struggled to remember but his mind
would not think.

At Bletchingley he noticed laughing, quarrelling children – like sparrows –
scrambling and sliding on a grassy slope. Their play was an excess,
a cup overfilled by a drunken god. Dread drained his mind
giving thought no entrance.

At Nutfield words shuddered to memory. Through a distant telephone
she had spoken slowly, as if learning new words, unsure of their sense.
He stared in astonishment at colours drenching stretched trees. She said:
'Will you come now?'

Leaving Redhill he looked for a bus stop. The world unknowing,
was usual and went about its business of buying bread and
creosoting its sheds. It stunned with sustaining rituals:
theirs were gone.

Walking down the drive at Earlswood to the maternity wing, he noticed
a puzzled snail meandering a way across the paving stones.
'Baby Andrew has died.' So leaving the school, he arrived to be with her
and their three-night new son –

Who was no longer there and, in a sense, no longer theirs.
Then epiphanies were scrubbed from their lives. In Godstone churchyard
over a white shoebox, they planted clumps of cowslips. Yearly they renew;
symbols infiltrating their lives; helping them breathe.

Derek Webster
England

Change

She is gone ...
what more is there to say
when love is mute
and all the sensitivities
bemoan these lacking words:
    I love her ...

She so bright and warm
has slipped between
time and the subtleties
rounded by reason:
    I yearn for ...

Excuses never make
the clock return
to all that tenderness
which now is part of time:
    Come back now ...

Yet tides must turn
and sun, then moon, arise
as love will follow pain
and seasons muse on quieter years:
    We'll love again ...

As friends we'll clasp spring's joy
in changed reality to come.
and all your loss will be our gain
when we are newly changed:
And love again ...
    As friends ...

Giles Harcourt
England

Widow

Further than all seeing,
I watch gulls skim and skate
      at the tide's edge.

Beyond all hearing,
I listen as reeds pipe a descant to eternity
      from the marsh's edge.

Further than all touching,
I walk through yellow suns of sunflowers
      to the meadow's edge.

Beyond every fragrance
I smell spring's newborn greenness
      at the wood's edge.

Remote from any flavour,
I taste honey at brown hives
      by the field's edge.

When this dark watch ends,
And madrigals of crickets still
      at the grave's edge.

And when my time is ravelled out,
May I come where no chart can settle,
      to a shadow's edge.

There, stipple with glory,
Will you greet me. And no longer
      shall I be alone.

Derek Webster
England

A Death in the Family

I hated to see you in hospital,
        all those tubes,
and you so weak, so helpless,
I shivered and turned away
and stuffed my flowers into a jar.

Now you are gone, gone for ever,
        and the music at the crem.
        and all those long prayers,
        and all the flowers
        will not bring you back.
We can cry but we can't win.

It's like a door from this lighted house
        into the night
and once we go through, there's no return.

        God, if you are the God of Jesus.
        you take care of everyone,
        so take care of this one we loved.
        Jesus, you know that doorway;
        walk this way beside us.

Lord Jesus Christ, keep us close to you.

Bernard Thorogood
Australia

I Long to Grieve with All My Heart

I long to grieve with all my heart,
he was the closest one to me;
but there is one who takes my place,
it is her grief the world will see.

Within the coldness of my room
I tear at pillows, scream inside.
Beyond these walls I wear a mask
while others point, and some deride.

They do not understand, the love
that held us through the winter's gloom,
that painted colours in the spring,
that now I share an empty room.

O Lord you understood the one
who drew you water from a well.
You recognised her chequered life,
but offered love instead of hell.

I'm trapped and yet the love we shared
held beauty and was meant to be.
O God am I entirely wrong?
O hold me fast and comfort me.

Andrew Pratt
England

Today is Our Hannah's Birthday

Sweet sixteen and never been kissed,
never done drugs, never been blitzed'
and never played truant from school,
or broken the family rules.
Never had childhood diseases,
chickenpox, measles or sneezes;
or dangled a ring from her nose,
or scandalised folk with her clothes;
or played her recorder too loud,
or stayed out all night with the crowd.
Never had fights with her brother,
never talked back to her mother,
never wound up her old father,
never the least bit of bother.
What angel is this? You might say,
whose birth we remember today.
How wide of the mark you would be –
there's nought to remember, you see.
As parents condemned to ask, 'Why?'
This day we would like to deny,
imagining what might have been
to have it all over again.
This day's not for presents and cake,
a birthday, it's also a wake;
a doomsday when faith's not enough,
and God-talk is piety's bluff;
a day of despair and accursed,
a day that could never be worse;
a day when the sun never rose,
a day that the years cannot close;
a terminal day without cure,
a day of grief that is pure:
our baby stillborn – and still mourned.

Kim Fabricius
Wales/USA

My Dead Sisters

Aimee was born before me
Georgina was born after me
They are both lovely names

All of us had problems
My sisters were very ill
Georgina and Aimee didn't have a life
They didn't even come home from hospital

When Mummy had Georgina
I went to visit her in hospital
But Georgina wasn't here
She was in special care

Mummy was worried
I had a feeling in my head
That Georgina was going to die

If my sisters had lived
We would have taken turns
In the front of the car –
Me, Aimee and Georgina

My granddad would have loved them
My two sisters
He would picked them up
And played with them
Now they are together in the churchyard
And they are together in heaven.

Robert Fox (aged 7)
England

Child Grieving

Here, then, is the dreadful thing
That I was not allowed to see before:
The gaping grave
Into which, this time,
Will be consigned
The remnants of my mother's
Spent mortality.

I only sought to confront
The reality of death,
Knowing with the instinctive wisdom
Of childhood

That this is how
You assimilate experience
In order to move on;
But the adults,
Imprisoned in their own fears,
And assuming
That I wouldn't understand
The truths they could not face themselves,
Forbade it.

There is a dream-like unreality
In being with them both
Again
On an early summer afternoon.
Last time. I squatted on the sand,
Industriously manufacturing
Sandcastles,
While they sat motionless
On their
Ugly, grey, postwar
Utility blanket,
Watching.

In today's stillness
I arrange narcissi
In a marble vase for them
Instead; and when I turn to go,
This time
The wound will heal

Rosemary Parrott
England

In Bereavement

Now a roller-coaster ride
of soul churning emotion;
then tossed upon a grieving tide –
unnavigable ocean.

Others pray; I rage inside,
O God, what are they thinking?
I concentrate on how to hide
the fear that I am sinking.

Lost without a map or guide
where rocks of faith sound hollow,
on cross-fresh paths I slip and slide
to catch the God I follow.

Jenny Dann
England

Come Holy Spirit!

As we gather with aching hearts full of treasured and lasting memories of ....
May your healing influence comfort and sustain those friends who mourn today.
We praise you for all that the loved ones have been to each other. For the
mutual love and care of their unique partnership and for all the trust that grew
up between them – through their gaiety of mind and spirit – as they journeyed
together from darkness into light and as they revealed joy even amid sorrow.
Gracious God, we give thanks for the life of ....and for her/his delight in
serving you and most of all that she/he is now at peace. We rejoice in the
liberation of the human spirit; for God's justice and presence – enabling us to
be free, generous in praise, peace-loving and unafraid.
So Come Holy Spirit – Come!
Thanks be to God

Wendy Whitehead
England

Release

Letting you go
has set me free,
free to be me.
and yet it is the hardest thing
I have ever had to do;

Letting go
of you.

Pat Marsh
England

A Mountain Symbol Will Rise

When I first held my new-born son in my arms I can still remember my thought.
I thought of the Christian story of Mary, the mother giving birth to her son.
I was never close to Mary as most people I knew were, because my prayer life
was dialogue with my secret friend, the Christ. I was happy and thought about
her happiness.

He was the only child I was able to have. He was bright and sweet. I remember
his first set of questions. He stood on a chair, elbows on the table and hands
under his chin asked, 'How come my head is on my neck? How come I can't take
it off?' Oh the wonder of children, what great joy and heartache they can bring.

A phone call forty-six years later informed me he had suddenly died. He felt
tired, took a nap and never woke up.

This can not be. How is this possible? Believe it! Believe it? Yes he's gone! My only child has died. I want to talk to the doctor. What do I do? Who do I call? Oh God, I have to tell his children. It's night! Don't call them now, wait until morning. Oh my God, his son is making his confirmation. We have to be at the church early – when do I break the news? He has two sons and a daughter. We must have an autopsy. Why did he die?

Calm down; take a breath, one moment at a time.

We have a tree my husband and I planted with an altar of stone dedicated to Jeffrey. It is close to our bedroom window. A Mountain Ash seems fitting. This boy, man, always loved the ocean and a Mountain symbol will rise.

In the darkness there is light. God had gifted me with a phone call from my son three days before he died. We had been estranged for a while and his last words on the phone were 'I love you, Mom.' When thoughts would come 'I should of' 'could of' I have learned it is important to forgive myself for any shortcoming I might have had as Mother.

Can we think of death as just a change?
Can we think of life as lessons to be learned?
Can we forgive ourselves for whatever we regret?

The answer is 'yes' when I know and feel the 'Divine Connection' in the web of life.

Eleanore Milardo
USA

Afterwards (1)

There were snowdrops
shyly nudging spring,
and daffodils hinting
a flash of gold
when you left us
with no goodbye.

Now buds are eager
to spill their beauty
in the empty garden.
O flowers and coming seasons
heal our grief,
heal our grief.

Cecily Taylor
England

Afterwards (2)

When your world is so shaken
like a child's snow-filled globe
and every flake falls in a different place –
you know then
though the backdrop remains
that life can never be the same again.

And every time waking from sleep
you face this anew; for how long?
how long until the mind accepts?

But the heart asks a different question:
will it ever heal?
It has *known* from the first moment,
for that is where the ache is.

Cecily Taylor
England

And Now You're Gone
(Dedicated to Rosemary Taylor)

Losing our friend is hard,
Losing a partner is tough,
But when they take their own life
You feel you haven't done enough –
To help, to understand, to simplify their choices,
You can tell yourself that they were sick,
But you keep on hearing voices:
If you'd done this or you'd done that
They'd still be here today,
The thoughts, the guilt, the blame,
It just will not go away.
But there are so many facets
Each one has played its part,
We've done what seemed best at the time,
That felt right in our heart.

She has a vision and a plan
To climb up to the heights,
From shadowy gorge where she feels trapped
To pastures new where promise grows,
To make it if she can.
The path she has, it is so steep,
But this she feels she must complete.

The struggle's hard,
She stumbles much,
And finally she falls –
Into the arms of the God she loves
At peace she circles with the doves.

She's free to walk the dales again
His love has transformed all her pain.
She appreciates the gifts she has
How much she gave and what it meant.
Purpose is clear,
A life well lived,
Forever now she is content.

And peace will come to those who mourn,
And happy thoughts they will return,
Of times we've had, we've loved, we've shared,
That lead us to a brighter dawn.
We are so thankful to have known,
An angel who has cared.

Paul Taylor
England

Reaching Out

When you are talking
to a really old person
they seem to only
half hear and see you.

They look at you
as if you are just an outline of a person
that hasn't been filled in
and they only reply to your words
that have specific meaning to them.

And sometimes when you are leaving
they reach out and
grasp your hand or wrist really tightly
and hang on as if to something precious.
Then let go and sit back
eyes closed, worn out by the effort.

Geoffrey Herbert
England

One Year On
(for Meg)

One year on:
And friends who came to stand
Shoulder to shoulder
In the sudden shock of loss
Have long since moved on –
Leaving us alone,
You and I,
Silent partners in a
Slow dance with time,
As we weave our way between
The unexpected silences
And unaccustomed empty space,
Until we redefine their meaning.

One day soon,
Lifting my head
From my writing
To listen for the small sounds
Of time passing,
Although not comfortable
With your new place
So far away,
It will have become
The norm. And then,
If momentarily
The pain is more
Because it has grown less,
It is the way of things.

Rosemary Parrott
England

The Last Time
(To My Father)

So often it catches us out – the not knowing,
thinking the years to spare for saying and showing
all that we meant and felt.

Now I treasure the more that unsuspecting moment,
though looking behind
I find the pain of its memory growing –
the last time I saw you smile before your going.

Cecily Taylor
England

Tears

Thank God for tears,
the tears that flow unchecked,
that run in rivulets
down to the sea of God;
that have to merge eventually
with something larger than the self.

Thank God for tears,
the tears that bring release
for knotted nerves
twisted as sinews,
bringing a breathing out
beyond despair.

Thank God for tears,
and then beyond the tears,
beyond the hopelessness
that has to offer up the grief
till no more fall,
because no more can fall –

the tiny step that is a journey's start,
a slow step onward,
numb at first and seeming dead,
where haltingly, but gradually
one grassblade starts to grow
watered by tears;
somehow a kind of healing can begin.

Cecily Taylor
England

Expectancy

I look back on a moment of sheer happiness. I remember it clearly, although
it happened thirty-nine years ago. I remember the weather: sunny and warm,
and the place: a sloping daisy-spattered field. I remember what I was wearing:
a cotton dress patterned in blue and green with a broad collar, a voluminous
dress designed to cover the bump of my pregnancy, and failing.

But what I remember most clearly is how I felt. There were people around,
friends and family, but for a short while I sat alone on the grass. I thought about
the child soon to be born: of the mystery that he was and the joy he would be.
I understood in that moment, the meaning of the words in the best loved of all
psalms: 'My cup runneth over.' And for a while I longed for time to stand still.

The same feeling returns each year when the snowdrops begin to show. They are beautiful, pale, pure, demure, But they are just the beginning; soon there will be an explosion of loveliness: wild daffodils, primroses, wood anemones, violets, bluebells. They bloom and they die and Spring gallops by. I wish time would stand still with the snowdrops, at least for a little while.

A few weeks after my moment of joy all those years ago, my child was born, a son. We called him Benjamin and loved him dearly. After a few months he died.

Somehow the sadness of his death in no way diminishes my memory of happiness.

Anthea Dove
England

An Unusual Memorial Service

Peter (not his real name) was a young man with severe learning difficulties who lived in a home run by the Home Farm Trust. When he died, the funeral was held in his family's home town in another part of the country; but a memorial service in our church was requested for the benefit of Peter's 'other family', the people with whom he had shared his everyday life. As well as the residents and staff at the home, members of Peter's family and other residents' families attended.

The service began with refreshments – helping people to feel relaxed in the church environment, and also giving them an opportunity to look at the photographs and memorabilia of Peter displayed on a table in the worship area.

Song: All things bright and beautiful (led from the front with actions based on signing)

Reading of a poem written by a friend of Peter's

Prayer (with simple repeated response)

Song: The Lord's my Shepherd (Psalm 23)

Talk (using daffodils as a visual aid – see below)

Everyone was then given the opportunity to collect a daffodil (having the choice of either a bud or a full-blown flower) and to place it in a vase on the focus table. They then remained at the front of the church to sing (and dance) the song 'Lord of the Dance'.

The service ended with everyone greeting each other (this included a lot of hugging, crying and laughing).

The ethos behind the service was to move away from a wholly verbal presentation to involve doing and thinking at a more experiential level. Creating through group activity, plus allowing for individual choice, enabled feelings to be expressed.

The placing of a focus table allowed the reason for the service to be clearly stated and given a person focus, which could continually be referred to as a reminder. It also provided a means of receiving contributions to the event and of making prior preparation and explanation.

Daffodils were provided in bud and full flower. This gave a visual hint at a life lived to the full and a new life beginning; at remembering a full life 'cut down' when young and remembering a person who shone with life and enthusiasm for both meeting and departing.

The incorporation of sign language into the simple songs again allowed participation by all and a simple repeated response in prayer gives time for all to respond and feel part of what is happening.

In fact there is not so very much difference between this service and other funeral or memorial services in that they are all intended to bring us closer to each other, to the person that has died and to God. The way in which this is done has always to be adapted to those attending. Overall this implies a deep respect and love for those needing to be helped in their grief at the loss of someone they loved. Can we do less?

Jenny Dann and Denis Smith
England

Shining Like A Star

Paul gives a wonderful image for remembering loved ones who have died in Philippians 2: 14-16. This can provide a responsive call to worship in a memorial service or funeral service.

She shone like a star in the universe
A light that guided us in our darkness
She did not labour for nothing
For we hold on to her words
She rejoices in the presence of the Lord
So let us thank God and rejoice with her
Let us give thanks for the memory she leaves with us
A memory that shines like an eternal light

> In her life, she was a star
> a shining light in our lives
> filling us with joy and hope,
> guiding us through the dark.

In our minds she is a star
just briefly hidden by a cloud
but still there, looking down
with a smile upon her face.

In our hearts she is a star,
gone with the light of day
but she'll be back brighter than before
when the dark of night returns

To us, she is a star,
an eternal light in our life
and we know where she is
for heaven is the home of every star.

Richard Becher
England

Be Comforted in Your Grief

It is always important to remember that although we are conducting a funeral in the context of our Christian faith there are others who need to be comforted in their journey through grief.

Be comforted in your grief;
Be strengthened by a faith.
If it is in God, feel his comforting embrace.
If it is in Jesus, feel his healing touch.
If it is the Spirit, feel her guiding hand.
If it is in the Three, be comforted, healed and guided
But if you have no faith
Feel the love of those around you
And let their presence be your strength on your journey through grief.

and a Blessing to embrace everyone

If you have faith in God,
    may you feel the blessing of God within you
If you have no faith in God
    may you feel the blessing of friends around you
With or without faith,
    may you be blessed by the love that surrounds you.
Amen

Richard Becher
England

Lord, You Know Me Better Than I Know Myself

It can be a comfort at a funeral or memorial service to know that God knows us better than we know ourselves. God hears words we do not speak but only think and so knows our deepest thoughts and meets us when others believe we are lost forever. They don't hear what God hears or know us as well as God knows us. Psalm 139 inspires this hope.

Lord, you searched me,
 and you knew me
  like no-one else ever could.
You knew me when I sat
 and when I stood;
  when I slept
   and when I woke.
You perceived my every thought
 from afar
  for you knew me
   better than I knew myself.
You knew all my plans,
 and every word
  before it was on my lips.
You even heard the words
 I didn't speak
  but quietly thought.
You were always with me,
 behind me and before me,
  laying your hand upon me
   but your presence, Lord,
    was too good to believe;
     too much for me to understand.
But there is no escape
 from your Spirit;
  no hiding from your love
   for wherever I go, you follow
    whether I rise on the wings of the dawn
    or settle on the far shores of the sea,
     your hand reaches out
      so that now you hold me
       and comfort me
        like a long lost child.

Richard Becher
England

Graveyard Dance

Gravestones,
Huddled round the Church,
Bowing to each other,
Nodding off in the long sleep.
Trees spread branches
Wildflowers
Enrich the grass.
Birdsong signals life
And sunshine wraps
In quiet warmth
Perhaps in Hope.

But wait.
Gravestone sleep is passing
As each completes
Their bow before the other
To join the dance.
Clouds split,
And His Light shines
As history rewinds
To set free generations
Frozen in time.
"Dearly Beloveds",
Who made an early exit
From life's stage,
Surprised
To find themselves alive,
The script rewritten,
Snatching victory
From the villain.
Plague and hunger
Flee the scene
And mothers weep for joy
As children
Tug their apron strings,
And songs of praise
Fill earth and sky
Heralding the King
On Resurrection Day.

Hugh McKee
England

Bereavement

'They die forgotten as a dream
    dies at the opening day.'

No, it is not so.

The dream fades to nothing
but those we love remain in our hearts.

That smile remains, that turn of phrase,
    that unhurried voice, that calm.
You are present in all your influence,
    challenging, honest, wise.
You are here in your work,
    the plans you drew,
    the business you built,
    or the song you wrote.
You live in the children you taught,
    part of their education and so
    part of them always.
You are alive in the love we share,
    the love you gave
    which touched our hearts.
You are with us now in the freedom we enjoy
    through your service, your courage.

You are not a dream,
You are reality.
Part of us today and always.

Bernard Thorogood
Australia

Moribund

Old age, last page, mute rage
Antique, pipes leak, joints creak,
Talk sense? Long since, past tense
Dry bones, gallstones, low groans
Wheelchair, past care, despair
All day, decay, can't pray
So bored, implored, 'Why, Lord?'
Sunset, cold sweat, bed wet
Midnight, can't fight, last rite
Just fell, such hell. Farewell
Time's curse, none worse, 'Nurse, nurse!'
Deceased, released, at peace.

Kim Fabricius
Wales/USA

Nunc Dimittis

In silence
My soul is waiting,
Waiting for God.

Waiting.
Praying.

There is nothing else I can do.

I have poured out my love,
Nursed him,
Cherished him,
Helped him along his destined path.

I have laughed with him,
Wept with him,
Shared so much with him.

And now,
Now I can only wait
And pray
The silence is all that is left
To share.

In silence my souls is waiting.
In silence my soul is praying.

Lettest now Thy servant depart in peace
According to Your word.

Pat Marsh
England

After the Accident
(Elegy for Anne and Michael)

What good are tears –
the hot and sudden tears
that prick my eyes?
Nothing
      can bring you back
      endorse my disbelief.

What good are tears –
the hot and aching tears
that burn my cheeks?
Nothing
      can bring you back
      provide me sure relief.

What good are tears –
the hot and useless tears
that sting my lips?
Nothing
      can bring you back
      begin to heal my grief

when chance plays such a thief.

Cecily Taylor
Engand

Matthew 25

When Judgement comes
      In clouds descending,
Love finds its reward
For those who offered shelter
To those upon whom it rained.

For Love reveals
      Light never ending,
Bringing a judgement
To those who threatened darkness
To those they misunderstood.

When Justice reigns
      With Freedom ringing,
It gives dignity
To those who had lived in need
And those from whom they received.

Paul Friett
England

Brokeness

Where is my God

when it hurts too much
to even cry;
when my pulsing head is heavy
with a tiredness
far beyond the chance of sleep,
and the tangled threads
of my emotions
are pulled and stretched
beyond their natural limits
to the edge, the very edge,
of breaking point:
when they're locked
so tightly knotted in my head
that I dare not, dare not
even try
to let them go
for fear they may explode
and scatter shrapnel fragments of this pain
to wound and damage
others standing by.

Where is the love of God
when I am broken
with the heavy grief
of this poor damaged, fractured life?

Where is His love
When I need him so?

****
He is here, my child.

He is with you now

and he weeps.
He weeps, for you.

Pat Marsh
England

Son

On your first birthday
when you were critically ill
I cleared your airways
every thirty minutes –
willing you to live.

Ten years later
when I stepped
into the path of a lorry
You swung your small arm
across my body
to protect me.

At eighteen
when I read your terse note
telling me that you were gay,
I ached at the absence of
dear mum, love Tim –

but later, when we talked
and my throat was choked
with grief, you sat up all night
sucking out my lungs –
willing me to live.

Elizabeth Cambridge
England

In Each Moment's Quiet Rememb'ring

(Written for a memorial service for the Still-birth and Neo-natal Death Society (SANDS))

In each moment's quiet rememb'ring,
God, hear our prayer.
In the grief that has no ending,
God, hear our prayer.
In our lonely, anguished crying,
In our sad, regretful sighing,
In our living and our dying,
God, hear our prayer.

As we share our loving story,
God, be our strength,
Telling of its loss and glory,
God, be our strength.
Through the emptiness of grieving,
Through the comfort we're receiving,
Through the struggle of believing,
God, be our strength.

As we learn that love is giving,
God, grant us peace.
As we find new hope for living,
God, grant us peace.
In the wrongs that call for righting,
In the courage for the fighting,
In the gleams of joy delighting,
God, grant us peace.

Jan Berry
England

The Chapel

This is the hospital chapel.
It's very quiet and peaceful in here.
Dedicated to the patients and staff of the hospital
        by the mill-owners and miners who paid for it..
Dedicated on such and such a day, month and year –
Dedicated to the blessed relief of pain,
        to healing and compassion and service
Dedicated to dedication –
To be a place of peacefulness and quietness,
Where people can sit for a few moments
        after the strain of visiting a loved member of the family.
And for patients to come to on a Sunday morning for the service.

It's very quiet and peaceful in here,
        so that if there's a moment to spare,
A nurse or even a doctor, seeking refuge in tranquillity,
May make an unofficial entrance, unofficial or semi-official.
The little light burns in front of the curtains where the bread and wine
Are kept quietly, quietly bringing them to our attention.
When the service begins the altar candles are lit,
But in the meantime now, when the chapel is empty,
The sanctuary light flickers in the quietness of the chapel,
The chapel-light burns quietly in the theatres and wards of the hospital.

Forgive us, Lord –
Though we work in the place where you are still working
Among the people whom you love
        and with whom you have made your home,
We need this opportunity of recognising you in silence and in symbol
For all the times we encounter you in other places
And pass you by without acknowledgement.

Roger Grainger
England

A Mass of Candles

Candles have come to the Cathedral
flames are jigging in a draught
in the cold and February darkness
light lives

The light of the world come to the temple
eclipsing the hope of Simeon's wait
at the time of our Lord's presentation
as due

Candles led the eucharist procession
curlicues of incense build a framework
Revealing the curves of vaulting
Above

to make it real, unvisioned and
Unminded
like long-dead light seeking rest
reflected imagined formless
Trinity

candleflames are struggling to reach
freedom in unseen solid arches
to escape from what sustains them
before us

into an existence now denied them
like a foetus lured through birth
to unimagined structures of existence
beyond

each flame a nascent life consuming
the energy that feeds it, as it grows
it burns its own potential giving
away

its very self to light a path for others
whom it can never know. A sacrifice
to earth and heaven simultaneously,
a sign

flickering fluttering fidgeting
and overcoming darkness
by being only what it can become
when held

in a creator's hand. After communion
one may remember bread and wine
and Christ
but what remains is insubstantial
convicted of life

David Bunney
England

An Epitaph to My Parents

She was old
but her heart was as young
as a new-fledged song-bird
at the zenith
of its flight.

She had little education
yet her spirit was as willing
and as eager as a child's
on her first school
morning.

She was weary and in pain
but her soul will survive
when its spark is released
to that universal fire
to stay forever burning.

He died a hero
but he never fought in battles.
He forsook his career
as a soldier for her sake.
For her sake and his soul.

But they died in separate wards
on their golden anniversary.
They were jointly cremated.
May they be joyfully
re-united

Celia Snaith
England

A Prayer Service to Celebrate a Life for Women *

We gather in memory of ... a most loving, gentle person.

Prayer:

O God we are grateful, thankful and celebrate the life of ... . Her love, compassion and generous sharing was a mirror of your Presence. To watch her special love for children (or other skills) was to witness the Christ among us. Enlighten us to see that in the vault of memories lies the healing herb that renders pain less deadly: the remembering and reliving of our many moments of love. We ask this through Christ. Amen

An appropriate song

Readings: 1 Corinthians 12: 4 – 12

John 4: 5 – 14; 19 – 21; 23- 24

Stories of special women to be read by various people. We pray that their courage to name, claim and move with their vision may be shared by women and men of our time.

Mothers in families, you have named us and given us life.

All: Mothers move here with us.

Ruth and Naomi, your devoted love for one another renewed your faith in the working of the Divine.

All: Ruth and Naomi move here with us.

Mary Magdalene, you were the disciple to the disciples, sharing with them the first news of the resurrection.

All: Mary Magdalene, move here with us.

Catherine of Siena, you reconciled warring factions of state and church and we name you Doctor of our Church.

All: Catherine of Siena move here with us.

Rosa Parks, you sparked the Civil Rights movement in the South by refusing to give your seat to a white man and move to the back of the bus.

All: Rosa Parks, move here with us.

An appropriate song

Prayer:

Spirit of God you are life-giving spirit who sets us free. You are both promise and uncertainty, poverty and hope, comfort and challenge. Waken in us a spirit of joy that we may celebrate all that is good and human and especially today, all that is woman, all that is ... whose life we celebrate.
Amen

Blessing:

May you recognise in your life the presence, power and light of your soul.
May you realise that you are never alone, that your soul in its brightness and belonging connects you intimately with the rhythm of the universe.
May you have respect for your individuality and difference.
May you realise that the shape of your soul is unique and that you have a special destiny here.

Eleanore Milardo
U S A

* This celebration can be used as a basis for reflection especially by substituting the references to women where applicable according to culture and country.

A Prayer Service to Celebrate a Life for Men *

Opening Words: We gather today to remember ...
a son/husband/father, a loving person

Prayer:

O God,
calm us into a quietness
      that heals
            and listens,
and moulds our longings,
      our wounds,
            our wonderings
into a more holy
and human shape
Amen

An appropriate song

Readings: 1 Corinthians 15: 35 –44
John 4 5:14, 19 – 21, 23 – 24

A Prayer Psalm: Loss

Part of me is gone:
      what years of love and affection
      had fused in me as one
      has now been cut away

Response: O God hear us

My heart has been split
      by the stripping
      of what I've learned to feel
      as an integral part of my being.
By the surgery of separation
I've become an amputee,
Disabled by death.

Response: O God hear us

O Divine Healer of hearts,
      remind me daily not to expect
      a miracle of quick recovery.

Guide me as I stumble,
    blinded by my tears,
    limping along from the loss
    of the one I have loved.

Response: O God hear us

Teach me that even the physically impaired
    can again learn to dance.
Enlighten me to see
    that in my vault of memories
    lies the healing herb
    that renders pain less deadly:
    the remembering and reliving
    of our many moments.
And grace me with your regenerating presence
    so that I can begin again.

Response: O God hear us

A Time to Share Memories

An appropriate song

Blessing
(stand in a circle)

May you recognise in your life the presence, power and light of your soul
May you realise that you are never alone,
    that your soul in its brightness and belonging connects you intimately
    with the rhythm of the universe
May you have respect for your individuality and difference
May you realise that the shape of your soul is unique,
    that you have a special destiny here,
    that behind the façade of your life there is something beautiful,
    good and eternal happening.
May you learn to see yourself with the same delight,
    pride and expectation with which God sees you in every moment.
Amen.

Eleanore Milardo
USA

* This celebration can be used as a basis for reflection especially by substituting the
references to women where applicable according to culture and country.

Travel Towards the Dawn

*(including prayers for care-workers, relationships,
celebration of women, a communion service for community living)*

**Let us Dream
Let us Fly
Let us give Peace a Chance**

*Bangalore Initiative for Peace
south India*

Let His Dawn Light New Horizons

When a blind man came to Jesus
asking for the gift of sight;
in those first few anxious moments
he could only see faint light.
then the full truth dawned upon him,
broke through his eternal night.

When a widow, lost in grieving,
knowing that her son was dead,
followed, weeping, to his burial,
Jesus saw what lay ahead.
with compassion he approached her,
raised the boy up from his bed.

When the storm clouds of Good Friday
drained the light out from the sky,
broken ones who followed Jesus
could not see the reason why.
Only with the dawn of Easter
could their heads be lifted high.

When our lives are drowned in darkness,
when our faith is under strain,
we can also look to Jesus,
give to him our fear and pain.
Let his dawn light new horizons
as our hope is born again.

Tune: 8.7.8.7.8.7.

*Marjorie Dobson
England*

Never Full Grown

Thanks be that we are never fully grown.
Each day, each month, each year
Gives time to be regenerated.

God of creation and re-creation,
You planted in us the seeds of life and growth
And challenged us to effort and to energy
That they might grow in us.

Enabling God,
By your continuing challenge,
     may we still grow
     in vision and in our use of your gifts
By your love and goodness,
     enrich and deepen our commitment
By your gifts to those around us
     and the insights that we share,
     may we be instruments of your blessing to one another.

Wendy Ross-Barker
England

I Don't Really Comprehend

I don't really comprehend
the way you think or what you say;
but you are a child of God
blessed with love, within God's sway;

Valued for the hidden grace
you do not know, you cannot show,
grace that's hidden from my eyes
grace that God can realise.

So I'll value you my friend;
each day I'll seek to understand:
how to learn and share with you,
take my learning from your hand.

Then together we will grow,
together we will reach for hope
far beyond our wildest dreams,
yet within God's boundless scope.

Andrew Pratt
England

When I Pray to You for Help

When I pray to you for help, O God
Do I hope that you will intervene,
Treating me as powerless as a child
Who can do no more than kick or scream?
As a human being come of age
Help me to work with you to earth each dream

We can work together with your power
As we trust the Christ who dwells within
Every human being's deepest self
And in whom all life is kith and kin –
For the energy that moves the stars
Is the same that breathes within our skin.

You are neither ill-disposed nor deaf
Yet we think we need to change your mind,
Urging you to listen to our prayers
Though our hearts are careless and unkind.
Help us change our rigid ways of thought
And embrace what each of us can find.

In the flow of life's great cosmic stream
We can find the loving which transforms.
As dependencies release their hold
We emerge from thinking which deforms,
To discern your just and loving peace,
Peace and growth for life in all its forms.

W L Wallace
Aotearoa New Zealand

If I Had the Power

If I had the power
to change the earth,
enemy
wouldn't be
in a dictionary.
I'd turn war into peace:
friendships
would never cease.
I'd wipe weapons out
and everyone
would shout out
with joy.
Global warming
wouldn't make the earth hot.
Animals would live
side by side:
from humans,
other creatures
would not have to hide.
Endangered creatures
would always be here.
The end of peace
would never come.
That's what I would do
If I had the power.

Hannah Warwicker (age 10)
England

My Boy

Let me give him
Schwarzenegger for strength
Einstein for brains
Nureyev for agility
Solomon for wisdom.

Let me teach him
pleasure in aims
pleasure in work
pleasure in sport
pleasure in life.

Please let him
know responsibility
enjoy humour
build self-reliance
show sensitivity

May he never know drugs
May he always know love.

Written in a Poem Workshop
St George's Crypt
Leeds
England

On the Road to Calvary

The cripple will walk to the mountain,
the blind man will come to see,
The leper will mix with the people,
going to Calvary.

Chorus: Stand up, be clean, open your eyes to the world I say,
laugh, leap, dance and sing, then follow the Lord all the way.

The blind man was sitting and begging
when Jesus was walking nearby,
he called 'let my eyes look upon you'
and Jesus took heed of his cry.

Chorus:

The cripple was dropped through a ceiling
as Jesus was teaching beneath,
his friends knew that Jesus could heal him
and he walked in the power of belief

Chorus:

The woman had waited for ages
for Jesus to pass somewhere near,
to touch just the hem of his clothing,
by faith she was cured from her fear.

Chorus:

The leper was shunned by his people
until he met Jesus one day,
by a touch he was healed and forgiven
and sent to the Temple to pray.

Chorus:

The cripple will walk to the mountain,
the blind man will come to see,
the leper will mix with the people,
going to Calvary.

Chorus:

Tune: My Bonny Lies over the Ocean
Colin Ferguson
England

The Counsellor

Today I met my friend,
The Counsellor.
Repeated reluctance,
Initial nervousness,
Gave way to silence –
Relief in me.

The tactful smile,
Appropriate word,
Prompted stirrings of new life –
Observed, this time,
From a different,
More daring perspective.

Use the crisis positively,
Creatively maybe?
Expectantly waiting
Clear vistas to appear.
Fear not to die a little
Sweep away bruised fruit and fallen leaves.

Weather a future storm
Confidently as the evergreen
Retain your dignity;
Let go – move on
With God, our friend,
The Counsellor.

In fond embrace, I trusted her;
Adventurously – stepped through the open door
To cherish the hearing just begun.

Wendy Whitehead
England

People Who Continue to Care

Friend and Saviour, we rejoice when we are blessed with good neighbours.
We thank you for all those people who continue to care – in unexpected and imaginative ways – even when it's inconvenient for them and when practical care proves costly.
For young and old who freely share their artistic and creative gifts with those who welcome them and often find them therapeutic
– we give you thanks.
For ready-listeners like Mary – whose care and counselling was valued by Jesus and for Martha's hospitality
– we give you thanks.
Renewing God by the leading of your Holy Spirit, teach us to be sensitive to the needs of others.
May each one find through your gift of grace the reality of strength in weakness.
Loving God, wash the feet of all your caring friends for whom to serve you is perfect freedom.

Wendy Whitehead
England

A Prayer for Carers

Caring God,
Strengthen, we pray, all carers –
those who daily shoulder responsibility
for the well-being of a vulnerable relative or friend.
May they be given appropriate support for their task;
may their needs and concerns be heard;
and may we all work together
to build a community where everyone
is treated with compassion and respect.
Through Jesus Christ our Lord,
Amen.

Jenny Dann
England

A Thanksgiving for Care-Workers

Reader One: Loving God, we praise you for prayer that heals. We praise you for your protection and watchfulness. Enable us to be more forgiving and make us aware of your closeness so that we become ever more caring.

Reader Two: Life-giving God, we thank you for all those whose work demands much giving of themselves and so much love. Thank you for their courage, cheerfulness and perseverance. Support them with the gift of your love, we pray.

Reader One: Vulnerable God, we thank you that you understand the problems of those who feel rejected or socially isolated. We pray for the physically abused and inwardly scarred – we ask for an easing of their pain. May those called to care for them or to pray for their future well-being, be encouraged by positive responses to their efforts or through recognised answers to their prayers.

Reader Two: Equip those whose job it is to care for the many people who, often through no fault of their own, find it difficult to help themselves. Strengthen, in the power of your Holy Spirit, those care workers trying to stimulate a response from people with learning difficulties or victims of strokes and those numbed by bereavement.

Reader One: We bring to you all relatives caught up in long-term caring of people suffering dementia. Help them grow in patience; may they not be tested beyond human limits and strengthen them through the power of prayer.

Reader Two: Be with those living or working with people damaged by alcohol or drug-related problems or struggling with AIDS. Spirit of the living God, relieve their weariness; renew their hope and perseverance. Open channels of communication and stir within them a desire to seek renewal and to be touched by the peace that passes all understanding.

In the name of Christ the Healer, we bring our prayers.
Thanks be to God
Amen

Wendy Whitehead
England

Comforter
(A Hymn for Carers)

When our caring love wears thin,
when our nerves are stretched and taut
and the strain of our concern
fills our every waking thought –
God of understanding hearts
give us strength to play our part.

When we watch in helpless love
when all hope of health is past
and distress cries out in pain
that this suffering will not last –
God of healing, hold us near,
Bring your calm and drive out fear.

When our tears speak out our love,
when by smiles we mask our grief,
in those dark and lonely hours
when the silence mocks belief –
God of comfort, to our night
Bring the dawning of your light.

* When the one we loved has gone,
when death brings tormented peace,
as emotions swirl around –
sorrow mingled with release.
God of patience, bear our pain;
Turn us back to life again.

Tune: Lucerne Laudonie 7.7.7.7.7.7.
* The last verse may be omitted if inappropriate
Marjorie Dobson
England

Life is Getting Better

Imagine walking into
people's lives that you have never known.
Imagine the look they give you
as they work you out.
Imagine these are the people
you're going to see every day
until you get out of the nightmare.
Imagine your room
no bigger than a box-room.
Imagine your bed is
the only place
where you feel safe.
Imagine your neighbours
playing ear-burn music
through all hours of the
night.
Imagine how lonely
you would feel
now that you're all
on your own
but then
imagine one of your inmates
knocking on your door,
they've been in your shoes before.
Imagine the warm friendly staff
that help you
with all the problems you'll
meet as life goes on.
I don't have to,
I've been through it
and life is getting
better.

Jennifer Earthy
Via Nightstop, Shipley, England

Living with HIV and AIDS

Lord of all creation, you bring meaning out of chaos, light out of darkness.
We rejoice with those who live with renewed hope and give thanks for all
who work to bring an end to the epidemic.
May those of us living with HIV and AIDS always find acceptance and support
to live life to the fullest and make our unique contribution to the world.

Praise to you, Lord, who has given us life.

Lord, yours is the earth and its fullness, the world and all its people. We thank you for the diversity of humankind.
May those who hurt or oppress others merely because of who they are, grow in wisdom and understanding, seeing your likeness reflected in all creation.

Praise to you, Lord, who makes us one people.

Lord, in you justice and peace embrace.
May we work for a time when all enjoy the abundance of the earth's riches and the benefits of advances in medical research.
May we welcome and embrace those who feel strangers in a strange land.

Praise to you, Lord, who gives hope and freedom.

Lord, ever close to the broken hearted, may those who mourn find consolation and the sick find comfort.
Be close to those who wake this night in pain, loneliness, fear and dread.
Out of the depths we cry to you, Lord.

As those who keep the night watch look for dawn so, Lord, we look for your help.
May a cure be found,
May we live positively.
May we find love to strengthen us and free us from fear.
O Lord, our refuge and strength.
Amen

London Ecumenical Aids Trust
England

Red the Ribbon

Red the ribbon that we're wearing,
Red for danger threatening,
Red the symbol of God's Spirit
Prompting the concern we bring.

Christ we praise, the great Outsider,
Friend of friendless, friend of youth;
Fiery often yet forgiving,
Christ the Way, the life, the truth.

Red the blood that Christ is shedding,
Hanging there, despised, alone;
All his beauty gone, disfigured,
Bearing sorrows to his throne.

Greater works than his, Christ promised,
Would be finished in his Name,
Works of mercy, works of healing,
Strength for which we dare to claim.

Christ in glory, Christ among us,
Spread your gifts across the earth,
Best the gift which recognises
Every human soul has worth.

Red the ribbon that we're wearing,
Red for danger threatening,
Red the symbol of God's Spirit,
Prompting the concern we bring.

David Mowbray
England

I Stood Afar

I stood afar,
Could not lift up my eyes
Knowing your hands were outstretched
Just as they were before,
The time you touched me
Spoke the words of healing
Said 'be clean'.

Sensing your arms were open
Just as they were before,
The time you embraced me
Me, beyond the reach, an outcast
Suddenly met by the tender
Inclusiveness of your love.

I was used to people averting their gaze from me
But now it is me who turns my face from you
Unnerved by your disfigurement, your bruises,
The unhealed wounds on you the healer.

Is it your helplessness I cannot bear?
Your vulnerability which tears my heart?
Or is it that now
As you hang there
I know that you are indeed one of us
Sharing our pain and isolation,
Experiencing rejection, even doubt.

Then in terror of darkness I hear your voice
'Father!
In your hands I place my spirit'.
I dare to look up
And in that timeless moment of your death
I see.

Jill Fuller
England

Into the Light

As you emerge
Into the light,
Let there be
No looking back
To the black chasm
That formed you,
Nor the long shadows
That enslaved you
As you yearned
To be set free.

For what is
The dark night of the soul
If not a foil,
A measure
By which we learn to recognise
The glimpses
Of bright treasure
Which flare forth
From the turmoil of our daily struggle,
To supply a promise
Of the life that is to be?

Rosemary Parrott
England

God's Delight

Woman stooping, bent and burdened,
Eyes downcast towards the ground,
Jesus beckons you to freedom,
Lift your head and gaze around.
        Sister, you are God's delight,
        Tall and grace-full in God's sight!

Woman, drained of life's sweet forces,
Ebbing vital strength away,
Touch his robe, soak in his power,
Jesus makes you whole today.
        Sister, you are God's delight,
        Health and dignity your right!

Woman, trapped by expectations,
Plaster saint or duteous slave,
Jesus offers choice and challenge,
Break the mould, be bold and brave.
        Sister, you are God's delight,
        Live the life and fight the fight!

Woman, self-abasing, fearful,
Clinging to your Master's feet,
Set him free – he longs to raise you,
In new life your Lord to greet.
        Sister, you are God's delight,
        Shout God's praise with all your might!

Tune: Brushnorth or any other 8.7.8.7.7.7.

Gillian Collins
England

Hymn to Celebrate Ten Years of Women's Ordination

As Christ's body we move forward
In the God who sets us free
Hoping, longing, weaving, struggling
With outrageous liberty
Bread of heaven, bread of heaven
Feed us on the stony road.

Truth now leads us into action
For the wounded of the earth
We would comfort, we would protest
Labouring in the world's rebirth
Oil of healing, oil of healing
Smooth the hands that soothe the world.

God of Wisdom's shaded pathway
Guide our faith communities,
Shape our dreams, inspire our dancing
With love's generosity
Songs of praises, songs of praises
Channel God's strong greening power.

Tune: Cwm Rhonddda
June Boyce-Tillman
England

I Sing a Song of the Woman's Voice

I sing a song of the women's voice
Tender and strong and clear;
Of those who longed to attain the vote
Despite men's doubt and fear –
    And one was a housewife
    And one was a nurse
    And one was a mother who cared for ten
    But all of them dreamt of women's rights
    And I plan to be like them.

I sing a song of the suffrage cause
Firing the true and bold
To plan and work fulfilling the hope
Which they first dreamt of old
    And one had a garden
    And one baked the bread
    And one made the beds and one washed the floors
    But all of them planned for women's rights
    And I aim to be like them.

I sing a song of the suffrage Christ
Freeing the sexist mind;
Empowering women whom men abused [1]
In roles which men defined [2]
    For Mary and Martha [3]
    His mother, his friends [4]
    Whatever their status, race or wealth
    Were all of equal worth to the Christ
    And each was a child of God.

I sing a song of sharing power –
Song of new life for all –
The way to prize each other's worth
And heed the suffrage call
    Till women and men
    The children, the aged
    Of each race who live on the face of this earth
    May join the struggle for human rights
    And follow the prophet's call.

Notes:

[1]	John 8: 1-11
[2]	John 4: 1-41
[3]	Luke 10: 36-42; 11.5
[4]	Mark 15: 40-41; 16:1

W L Wallace
Aotearoa New Zealand

An Unnamed Woman

God of pain and fear,
do you feel the tears
falling as leaves to a barren earth,
decked in the splendour of Autumn's richness,
beauty masking their imminent death?

You were there long ago –
when a precious jar was broken,
its fragrant contents poured out,
an unnamed woman foretelling death,
her touch evoking intimacy,
her actions inciting dispute.

You keep vigil with us, waiting
As the long night draws in,
Trusting experience to the rhythms of life.
Anoint us with the touch of your intimacy,
Knitting together wounds too deep for words.
God of intuitive wisdom,
Grant us the maturity to offer extravagance
In the face of another's pain,
Evoke in us the memory of her story,
Weaving through the patterns of time.

Clare McBeath and Jill Thornton
England

On the Other Side

Beyond the edge
of yesterday's horizon
I stand expectant,
open, tired.

It is a place I longed to be
and yet
it still surprises me
in its unique different strangeness.

It was the very Everest
of mountains to be climbed:
the surrendering of that pain
into His love.
So long had it been part
of me.

I am so drained,
exhausted by the struggle.
I find myself
standing now
inside this new beginning,
carried across the threshold, as it were,
by the powerful love of God;

and yet
        needing still
                to wait,

to wait on God.

The time for energy, for synergy
is not yet here.

Now is the time for rest,
renewal, growth,
a moment to be cradled
in the comfort of His love.
Cradled

on the other side of the pain.

Pat Marsh
England

None Out-ranks Another

None out-ranks another
in the sight of God;
each must follow humbly
in the steps Christ trod.

Children or their parents,
adults, black or white,
all are placed as equal,
valued, in God's sight;

Rulers or their people,
atheist or saint,
rated high or lowly,
loved without restraint.

So we'll walk together,
take each other's hand;
race or creed won't matter,
side by side we'll stand.

Metre 6.5.6.5.
Andrew Pratt
England

You and Me

You saw the sun rising from the sea
I saw the sun rising from the mountains
We argued for a long time,
Until you visited me and I visited you.
We saw the different facts.
You say it's summer
I say it's winter
We argued for a long time.
Then you visited me in the South
and I visited you in the North.
We saw the different facts.
You say, 'white is beauty'
I say 'black is beauty'
We argued for a long time.
Then you saw the black forest in my country
and I saw the eternal snow on your mountain peaks.
We agreed that the beauty of white is in its clear brightness
and the beauty of black is in its mysterious darkness.
Sharing – face to face – friends we shall become
You and me.

C M Kao
Taiwan

Tapestry

(Written on the consecration of Gene Robinson, gay bishop,
of New Hampshire, USA 2 November 2003)

God weaves
the lives of men and women
into a rich cloth;

we can not see
the whole design
only fragments.

Today the tapestry
is worked with
a new, strong thread –

a vibrant colour
to catch the light.

Denise Bennett
England

Prayers for My Two Children Who are Both Gay

May they occupy a corner of your garden
where the sun is gentle;
allow them to grow in their own way.
Let them be themselves
unshackled, unconfined
but always, blood of the grape –
fruit of your vine.

Elizabeth Cambridge
England

Gay Children

I never thought
how much I'd ache

to read the words
from my daughter –

Dear Mum
please tell Dad and my brother ...

Or the hand written scrap
from my son –

Dear Mum
there is no easy way to say ...

I never thought
it would take four years

to place pictures of them
with their partners

in frames
in the sitting room –

or the joy I would feel
seeing them set in silver.

Elizabeth Cambridge
England

Prayer Card
(Hereford Cathedral)

In the cathedral
she seeks the comfort of candles,
lights one for her daughter,
one for her son.

As children
she always gave them
the choicest pear, the ripest plum.
Now they have grown
she stands like a chalice
drained of wine,
watching the yellow flames fan.
In her heart
she moves her hand.

Elizabeth Cambridge
England

Letting Go

I am the raft you reach for
the rock you cling to
the rope which hauls you in.
I am the door you open
the arms which hold you
the bread you eat each day –

but there will be
another raft
another rock
another rope to haul you in.
There will be another door
for you to open,
and other arms to hold you –

but you will always be
the bread I eat each day.

Elizabeth Cambridge
England

Looking Forward

Each night
I light a candle
for my grown-up children.
Make a wish.

May you not bark your shins
or hurt your hands,
May all the storms in your heart
be small.
May you remember
that in the bright dazzle of this world
all that glisters is not gold*

May you smile with your arms,
embrace with your eyes.
May you know that all your
tears of joy and grief
have made space for life and love
to flow –

and may you grow strong enough
to sing with your feet.

* The Merchant of Venice - Shakespeare

Elizabeth Cambridge
England

Family

This is the classic pose, mother and daughter close.
I am ballooned in flowery smock, she is two,
Newly woken from sleep. She turns her questioning eyes
To the lens, sucking her fingers fiercely, to the bone;
Leans her head against my breasts.
And tucking her knees under the rim of my belly
She listens to the sound of her brother's heartbeat.
I am brimming with love. See how her dad
has captured her tousled black bob...

Outing

...Sixteen years on and I am out of the frame.
A fun snap taken at a pub shows two smiling girls
Arms entwined, confronting the camera.
It's been years since we clung like this,
Her tiny, ivy-hands star printing my bare flesh.
Through my filmy gaze she gathers the girl
With the unbraided Rapunzel hair
To her breast. Look how the semaphore
Of her arms bravely signals love.

Elizabeth Cambridge
England

Waiting on the Sofa

Debbie came to us today;
She smiled as she came through
She waited on the sofa
- I thought through what to do.

Hadn't made her room up
Supper not prepared
She waited on the sofa
- I don't think she cared.

'Would you like a pizza?'
(No teenager says no)
she waited on the sofa
- I got it on the go

'And what about some garlic bread?'
a smile and then a 'Yes!'
she waited on the sofa
- didn't show me her distress.

Her mother had said 'don't come back';
Last night, she slept outside.
She waited on the sofa
- inside, I think she cried.

Whenever there's no comfort
I know I should be there
So those waiting on the sofa
Can know that someone cares.

Jean Rahman Dalrymple
Via Nightstop, Shipley, England

The Lost Child Returns
(Luke 15: 11–32)

She's coming home!
She's coming home!
The long lost child,
is coming home again!

She travelled far
  dancing and singing
    to life's sweet music;
      laughing and spending,
        living life to the full
          but giving as much
            as she took out of life.
She travelled far
  and met with despair,
    laughter disguising
      her sadness and pain,
        protecting her friends
          from the goodbye
            to come
              as she sets off for home.

None of us are worthy
  to be called children of God,
but all of us can serve
  in the Kingdom to come.

God, the broken hearted Father,
  sees from a distance
    the long lost child
      his heart dancing with compassion
        as he runs to greet her,
          with a forgiving kiss
          and a loving embrace.

She's home! She's home!
  The long lost child
    is home again.

Only God hears
  the words that she speaks:
    Father, forgive me
      I have sinned against you
        I'm not worthy of your love,
          but please let me serve you.

God, the forgiving Father,
  gives her the best robe,
    puts a ring on her finger
      and shoes on her feet
        then sends for the food
          for a celebration feast.

She's home! She's home!
  The long lost child
  is home again ...

Richard Becher
England

A Creed from an Urban Community in Britain

We believe in God who made the world,
        loves it and laughs at it.
Who created human beings each to be different
        and asked them to get on with each other,
Who took the risk of leaving us alone,
        knowing that one day our differences
        might become a threat to the earth's safety.
Who trusts us with full knowledge of our frailty.
We believe in Jesus Christ, who came among us insignificantly,
Who grew among us uneventfully, who walked among us incognito;
Who to change the world, became redundant and called others to do likewise;
Who befriended those whose company would discredit him,
Who pardoned those who were hopeless cases,
Who spoke the deepest truths in the language of the living room,
Who contradicted common sense
        by accepting the cross and taking on the grave
        and was liberated on the third day.
Who calls us now, as then, to a life which is absurd
        by the standards of the world.
We believe in the Holy Spirit through whom God surprises,
        disappoints, cajoles and questions us;
Who is the bringer of strength and source of humour,
Who leads us to discover the truth we avoid,
Who is a paradox ... ever present yet predictable;
And we believe that the foolishness of God is wiser
        than the wisdom of the world
And we rejoice that God has made it so.

Source Unknown

A Little Lower Than God
(Psalm 8:5)

This prayer could be spoken by different voices from different parts of the church with plenty of silence between each question
First, read the whole psalm as a prayer.

Little lower than God?

Does this include the street children looked on as pests in some South American cities?

Silence

Does this include the people who are refugees to this country, including those who are hoping for a better life even though they could survive in their homeland?

Silence

Does this include those who are different in religion and culture to me and you?

Silence

Does this include those who are heterosexual and those that are bisexual and homosexual?

Silence

Does this include the people who are victims of injustice in society and paralysing poverty?

Silence

Does this include the lepers that Jesus touched and the prostitutes he embraced and the foreigners in whom he saw so much of God who is way beyond being merely Hebrew?

Silence

God, present and hidden in each person, help me to see you in the beauty and ugliness of the other.

Help me to look on others like you dare to look on me.
Amen.

John Ll Humphreys
Wales/Scotland

Deep Community
A Communion Service

Let this service be conducted informally with a circle of people around the table. If the service is to be held in a room with pews, people should be close to each other. One loaf (or roll of bread) and common cup(s) are appropriate.

The service assumes there has been the reading and proclamation of/reflection on the scriptures.

Be flexible about the order in which the elements of worship are introduced. Be conscious of sights, sounds, touch, smell and taste which will also contribute to the atmosphere of worship.

'Voice' indicates a single speaker, preferably not the same person throughout.

Gathering Around the Table

Voice: So many people are invited here, drawn here because there is friendship, welcome and belonging here. We are invited because we are the focus of love which is Divine. God is within each and because God is within each, God surrounds each. Our breath is the Spirit of the Holy.

In silence, hear each other, hear God's breath.

Invite silent prayer: who is the neighbour I find it difficult to imagine at this table?

Voice: Let's welcome each other to this gathering place.
May God help us overcome any sense of our own worth rejecting the worth of another.

All: **There can be no one unwelcome. We have no right, authority or desire to turn anyone away!**
We give each other a sign of welcome and a touch of peace.

The people gathered share the peace or say the grace to each other.

Voice: We don't come because we have the right to be here. We come because we're wanted here. We want each other and sense the wanting of God. How we are, how we feel towards one another is a glimpse of God's feeling towards us seen in Jesus.
It is a divine, embracing and limitless act of community to discover we are each and all drawn to eat, drink and accept love here.

Deep Community

Voice: At the heart of the Jewish faith lies the ancient understanding of the Hebrew people that they were rescued from harsh slavery by a God who listened to their plight. Moses and Joshua led them to the Promised Land. It was God.

When Jesus sat for what we call the Last Supper with the women and men who were his closest companions and friends, they thought on Moses and Joshua. And at the Passover of the Last Supper the land of Palestine was occupied, yet again. There was no freedom in the Promised Land. Some expected a fantastic release from this occupation.

Voice: Jesus talks about the meal as life. It is a meal to celebrate life. Jesus speaks about giving himself because life is so important. This is not to persuade God that life is important. Jesus knew that God already showed that as he sprung out of almost everything and everyone that Jesus saw! The sower, the mustard seed, the farmer, the servant and the unjust steward, were for Jesus stories about God. The prostitute, the poor, the untouchable, the foreigner and so many more who were the least of his sisters and brothers and in whom Jesus found it so obvious to look for what God is like.

Voice: This meal is cruel. We know that life has cruel, painful and distorting moments. Crucifixion is close. There is a highly charged emotion. How intimately Jesus offers his friends food. Through generations of welcome and rescue from isolation and destitution food has been a constant symbol of the good host and acceptance.

Voice: We know, too, that life is meant for living to the fullest possible measure. This means that the richness of life is expressed very differently by each of us. We are different people; we grew differently. The depth of community, the prophetic nature of our community is that God who is at the centre of our being speaks through each person to be met more fully by our being together.
The meal is one in which we receive the welcome of God, the trust of God and the commitment of God. This meal is the example of how the whole of human life can be.

Breaking Bread

Voice: **The Words of Institution – 1 Corinthinas 12**

Voice: These are not words to make us cower. They are the down to earth giving of one individual to another, the giving of God to you. The invitation is open; the purpose is to make us look at each other and at the world with love, hope and faith.

Bread is a basic commodity for life. Food is vital. Jesus spoke of himself as food, not physical food but nourishing commitment of God.

There is hope. Life becomes richer. Our communities become more just, people are embraced. Here and now, in this sharing, the divine welcome, the community of God has already begun.

Look at this bread and wine. There is a wonderfully Divine moment. To receive is to say God's yes to each person. There are no exclusion zones around this table. There are no requirements other than to want to say yes to the divine invitation and celebrate the life of Jesus.

Leader: Mysterious God, deep at the centre of each of us, reaching out from each, enable us to be a gathering in which there is a genuine demonstration of community, as you sought community amongst the rough gathering of Hebrew slaves walking to an unknown and sometimes frightening future. As they saw your being in and with them because of manna and sustenance on their journey, so too, let us see that the bread and wine on this table are signs for us that the journey is with you, for you and in you.

As we share bread, we remember the fact that in Jesus we are shocked by the power of your love for all human beings.

As we drink this wine we remember that you, holy, mysterious God are not remote, not 'out there' like some strange alien. We remember Jesus' life, after Jesus' death and the experience of Jesus' being as the visible likeness of the invisible divinity at the heart of every child, woman and man in the richness of our diversity.

All: **The Holy God within us demands that we speak well to and of each other. The Holy God around us in our communities of work, rest and play celebrates the kaleidoscope of humanity. This wonderful God speaks well, blesses, rejoices in each and looks for that shalom. The peace with justice where we can each rejoice because of the other and rejoice because we are each embraced.**

Voice: I take this bread to be food for life. I take it to share its life with my communities.

All: **We take this bread because the God in Jesus is the God in us.**

The bread is passed on from one to another or distributed as appropriate to the room and it's furnishings (similarly the wine). Explain how this is to be done so that all feel comfortable.

Voice: I take this wine symbol of blood, the life which rushes through all life. It is the life of Jesus.

All: We take this wine because the God in Jesus is the God in us.

Silence

Voice: Let's look at each other.

What does God see?

The present, future, and hope of humanity!

All: Let's go and be
a people of grace
a people of hope
a people of justice
a people of love

A people for the world
A people for God
Let's go!

John Ll Humphreys
Wales/Scotland

Forgiveness for Walking on the Other Side of the Road
(Prayer for the Campaign Against the Arms Trade)

Dearest compassionate and loving heavenly Father
Let the Campaign Against the Arms Trade be guided and blessed
by your wondrous self.
Dearest forgiving and loving Father
We seek your forgiveness for walking on the other side of the road
And ignoring the arms trade and its effects upon the world.

Most Holy, Holy, Holy and Wise God
Please open the eyes of those in the arms trade and show them
Where else they can direct their skills and use their knowledge
And also let them do that which is just and right in your eyes.

Our radiant, glorious and wise Lord God
Let it be revealed to us how to remove the burden caused by the arms trade
From those strangled by debt throughout your world.
Again we ask that Campaign Against Arms Trade
Be guided and blessed by your wondrous and magnificent self
And we plead in your mercy you will cleanse us of the innocent blood
upon our hands.
This we ask in the name of your Son, Lord of Lords and King of Kings
Jesus Christ

Clive Bates
England

Dreamer at Prayer

God of creation, Designer supreme
Our sensitive weaver of action or dream
  With praise we adore you; we feast on your gaze,
  Endearing, unending, O radiance of days.

To God of the workplace, to God of all skills
We bring our thanksgiving, we offer our wills,
  With you and your colleagues, let's work with our hands
  To love and to cherish; to pray for all lands.

God of all unions, all parties, all creeds
Bring us to new life through being, not deeds
  In the name of the Godhead, the Spirit, the Son
  As God's healing leads us, may all become one.

God of the Cosmos, great God beyond time,
When limits beset us, or sorrow or crime,
  Be close to support us; ordain us as thine
  Through grace and through wholeness may forgiving light shine.

Part II

  God of the landscape, dear God of all life,
  May you, our provider, forgive us for strife
    For those who face drought and daily distress
    Let your spirit guide us, the needy to bless.

  God of the flatshare, the commune or home,
  We pray for the rootless, wherever they roam,
    Whatever their story, whatever our song,
    Lord, bring us together – that all may belong.

  God of all certainty, God of all trust,
  Please take our confusions and turn them to dust,
    Relieve us of stresses – your hope to reveal
    As seeds of renewal we discover will heal.

  Source of humanity, help us to see
  The vision of peace is ours to foresee;
    Remake us and mould us – your dreams to review
    Let your vision guide us true faith to pursue.

Wendy Whitehead
England

Healing Hands

Have you known the healing hands of doctors?
Of nurses, confident, serene?
Have they been a source of comfort?
Supportive listeners,
Ready to reassure –
Each time to dare to dream.
Praise God for healing hands;
The skill, commitment, kindness, they express.
May those who've found such healing
Reach out to thank and bless.

Wendy Whitehead
England

A Christian Ministry

For those who through word and deed bring true humanity to relationships and show compassion to the needs of others:

Let us bless the Lord.
Thanks be to God

For those whose thoughts turn into prayer and whose prayer turns into action; Let us bless the Lord
Thanks be to God

For those who show forth the gifts of the Spirit in love, joy, peace;
for those who are patient, good, gentle, self-controlled and faithful;
Let us bless the Lord.
Thanks be to God.

For those whose love bears all things, hopes all things, endures all things,
whose love never ends;
Let us bless the Lord.
Thanks be to God.

Thomas Morton-Johns
John Tiernan
Prisons Week Committee

Come to Us

Sweet Sophia
Protector of our souls.
Enfold us with
The wings of your Spirit.
Quieten us
Renew us.
Your presence to comfort us.
Your healing to anoint us.
Your love
To reassure us.
Come to us
Sweet Sophia
Protector of our souls.
Enfold us with
The wings of your Spirit.

Follow me
follow me
close to me
now
Breathe on me
breathe on me
breathe on me
now
Touch for me
touch for me
skin to mine
now
Live with me
live with me
life within
now.

We come to you divine and holy One
    to feel your breathing
    to taste your food for our souls
    to hear your sweet words of tender love
    to see your likeness within ourselves
    to smell the pungent aroma of your presence.
For you are with us
Today we dream –
and you are here.

Colleen Geyer
Australia

Blessing

We are all on a journey through life
towards wisdom;
encountering each other through struggle;
honouring each other in celebration and
in hope;
seeking to be a community together,
with all of humanity.

Let us go forth, to be all
that we have the potential to be
receiving the care and nurture of each other.
Sharing together with compassion
And friendship.

Together and apart, let us seek the wisdom of
God's love
And know that we are held by the power of the
Holy Spirit,
To love and to walk gently on this earth.

Christine Cargill
Australia

A Collective Blessing

To be at peace, let us respect one another.
The only time we must look down on someone
is when we bend down to lift up the other.

Amen

Source Unknown

Index of Authors

Index of Authors

Index of Titles

To Become More Aware

Discovering Ourselves

Becoming A More Responsible People

Scene Changes

Living Our Difficult Days

Resourceful and Resilient

A Sri Lankan Journey

Reflections on Memories and Bereavement

Travel Towards the Dawn

Acknowledgements and Sources

To Become More Aware

All are Welcome © John Ll Humphreys

Birth Brings a Promise of New Life Awaking, Marjorie Dobson © Stainer and Bell Ltd
Blessing for Someone Living with Alzheimer's, A, Marjorie Dobson © Stainer and Bell Ltd
Bosom Friend © Hira Bansode

Children of God © Wendy Ross-Barker
Confession on the Road © Janet Lees
Contact © Cecily Taylor

Dancing Man © Paul Friett
Dear Mum © Elizabeth Cambridge
Discovering Respect for One Another © Nicholas Colloff

Excluded © Jean Palmer

Father Forgive © Ecumenical Forum of European Christian Women
For St Botolph's – Aldgate – London © Paul Friett

Grandchildren © Cecily Taylor

I'm A Kid © Kim Fabricius

Inclusion © Dipti Bhatia
In Memory of All the Women, © Jan Berry from Encircling Prayer
Insight © Frances Ballantyne
In the Depths of Silence – Source Unknown
It is High Time We Decided © Frances Phillips, Jesuit Refugee Service, Uganda

Light in Darkness © Wendy Ross-Barker
Listening God © Heather Pencavel
Love was Born © Wendy Ross-Barker

Mayan Prayer © Julio Quan, Source Unknown
Missionary Encounters © Anne Richards
Modest Yet Mutinous, Striving for Justice, Andrew Pratt © Stainer and Bell Ltd
Moment Catcher © Zico

NFA, © Colin Ferguson

Poem, © Teresa Larkman

Post-modern Case History © Cecily Taylor
Prayer for Regions and Nations © Heather Pencavel
Prayer for Trade Unions © Heather Pencavel
Prayer of a Desperate Parent, A © Zam Walker

Report from the Front © Diane D'Souza
Running Out of Food © Wendy Ross-Barker

Sexuality, Ranjini Wickramaratne-Rebera © In God's Image Vol 20 No 3
September 2001, Journal of Asian Women's Resource Centre for Culture
and Theology. Permission Sought.
Sounds of Silence © Hannah Warwicker and Janet Lees
Stan © Roger Grainger
Stranger, The © Margaret Herbert
Stretch Out Your Hand © Wendy Whitehead
Sunset, Marjorie Dobson © Stainer and Bell Ltd

This is the Room © Elizabeth Cambridge
Today Tomorrow © Margaret Alford.

Water is … © Hannah Warwicker and Janet Lees
What is God Worth? © Jenny Spouge
Where is God Today? © Heather Pencavel
Where is Justice, A Malaysian Woman © In God's Image Vol 21 No 3 September
2002, Journal of Asian Women's Resource Centre for Culture and Theology.
Permission Sought.

Discovering Ourselves

Accompanied All the Way © Norm S D Esdon
Affirmation of Inclusiveness, An © W L Wallace
As for the Grass © Janet Lees

Blessing of the Bizarre, The © John Hunt
Blind Abseiling © Colin Ferguson
Butterfly, The © Jenny Spouge

Caged Bird © Pat Marsh
Charity? © Paul Friett

Dad, I want My Stabilisers Back On © Hugh McKee
Detention © Cecily Taylor
Discoveries © Cecily Taylor

Faith Encounter © Wendy Whitehead
Fingerprints © Pat Marsh

Hear Me, Dear Lord © Colin Ferguson
Hey, This is Me © Pat Marsh

I am Not Alone © Tiny Powell
I Can Sing Your Goodness © Margaret Herbert
I Know a Boy © Cecily Taylor
I'm Not Just A Back © Geoffrey Herbert

Lonely Out Here, Cecily Taylor © Stainer and Bell Ltd

Moods © Marjorie Dobson
Mothering God, Marjorie Dobson © Stainer and Bell Ltd

No-one Can Share My Inner Space © W L Wallace

O Christ, within Your Heart and Mind © W L Wallace
On Being A Woman © Diane D'Souza
Open to Me © Rene Philombe

Personal Creed, A © Celia Snaith
Prayer for God's Blessing on A Homosexual Union, A © Gail Ramshaw

Retirement, Marjorie Dobson © Stainer and Bell Ltd
Roses at My Feet © Hugh McKee

Silence © Anasuya Sengupta
Soft Wounds of Brush on Canvas, Andrew Pratt © Stainer and Bell Ltd

Taking Measure © Diane D'Souza
They © Elizabeth Cambridge
Thirst © Cecily Taylor
Through All the Changing Scenes ... , Marjorie Dobson © Stainer and Bell Ltd
Time Matrix © Rosemary Parrott
Two Sides to a Coin © Paul Friett

When I Was Very Young © W L Wallace
Who Am I ? (1) © Elizabeth Tapia
Who Am I ? (2) © Ann Bedingfield

You Are Very Special © Source Unknown

Becoming A More Responsible People

Are You My Neighbour? Anonymous © Badelika Project, Kenya and Mildmay
Mission Hospital UK

Cry from the Desert Sand © M R Manohar

Help the Children ... © Hywel Nevard

I Could No Longer Support My Family © Christian Aid
I Have Called You By Your Name and You Are Mine © Janet Wootton

Lifeline, A © Christian Aid
Litany for the Children of War, A © Jan Berry
Litany for the World's Children, A © Heather Johnston
Lives Have Been Broken, Marjorie Dobson © Stainer and Bell Ltd
Look at People All Around, Andrew Pratt © Stainer and Bell Ltd

Motorist's Prayer, The © Geraldine Binnall

Pestalozzi © Pestalozzi International Village Trust
Original Source Unknown
Pray for Those who Suffer © Danielle and Naomi Bowdler
Prayer for the Peace of Humankind, A © National Christian Council in Korea
Prayer of Commitment to Non-violence, A © Campaign Against Arms Trade
Prayer of Confession, A © Claudia Genung Yamamoto
Prayer of Dedication, A © Church of North India
Psychological Trauma of War on Children, The © May Al-Daftari, Medical Aid for
Iraqi Children

Saying NO © Heather Pencavel
She is A Broken Child © M R Manohar
Sisters and Brothers in Chains © Alan Litherland

They Heal Their Bodies ... They Heal the Earth, Aruna Gnanadason © In God's
Image Vol 19 No 3 September 2000, Journal of Asian Women's Resource Centre
for Culture and Theology. Permission Sought.
They Will Come ... © United Reformed Church
Think It Over © Anil Kumar Patil
Those Who are Left Behind © Doreen Gazey
Time of Drought, A © Bernard Thorogood

Vulnerable God, Hear the Cries of Your People, Andrew Pratt © Stainer and
Bell Ltd

Wife Farms the Land, A © Find Your Feet

Scene Changes

Age Old Excuse, The © Richard Becher

Dangerous Games © Heather Pencavel
Departure Lounge © Pat Marsh

Eternal Life Found in a Rubbish Bin © Daniel Elias Fernandades, The Bible Society

God-controlled © Frances Ballantyne
God the Weaver, Marjorie Dobson © Stainer and Bell Ltd

I Want to Change the World © Joanna Margaret Paul

Litany of Freedom, A © Church of North India
Lives are the Currency Spent in War's Carnage, Andrew Pratt © Stainer and Bell Ltd

My Mother in Heaven, Wong Mei Yuk © In God's Image Vol 19 No 3 September 2000, Journal of Asian Women's Resource Centre for Culture and Theology. Permission Sought.

Persistent God, Marjorie Dobson © Stainer and Bell Ltd
Pray for a Big Change © Linda Jones/CAFOD
Prayer for Detained Asylum Seekers © Jesuit Refugee Service

Seven Happy Women © Traidcraft

Threshold © Pat Marsh
To Change it All – for Good © Wendy Ross-Barker

What Will You Do? © Cecily Taylor
Woman, You are Called, Bibiana Bunuan © In God's Image Vol 21 No 2 June 2002, Journal of Asian Women's Resource Centre for Culture and Theology. Permission Sought.

Living Our Difficult Days

Ballad of Maria Colwell, The, Cecily Taylor © Stainer and Bell Ltd
Balthazaar © Celia Snaith
Being There © Pat Marsh, from Bubbles and Rainbows and Butterfly Wings
Between Heaven and Earth © Richard Becher
Birthday, The © Cecily Taylor
Brought Through © Jan Berry

Camera Shot © Pat Marsh
Cancer © Kim Fabricius
Crisis in Hospital, A © Bernard Thorogood

Acknowledgements and Sources

DMDs? © Liz Burns
Depression © Derek Webster
Diagnosis © Margaret Alford
Dream or Nightmare? © John Grooms

Echoes, Marjorie Dobson © Stainer and Bell Ltd
Eric © The Raine Family

Face to Face © Wendy Whitehead
Fear © N Stevenson
Fling Wide my Door © Celia Snaith
Foothills © Pat Marsh

Good Samaritan, The © Pat Marsh from Bubbles and Rainbows and Butterfly Wings

Goodbye Van Gogh © Cecily Taylor

How Long, O God © Jan Berry

In Situations of Abuse © Zam Walker

Journey, The © N Stevenson

Let Us Reach Beyond the Winter, Andrew Pratt © Stainer and Bell Ltd
Living and Dying with HIV/AIDS © United Reformed Church
Losing the Fairytale © N Stevenson
Loss of Sight, Marjorie Dobson © Stainer and Bell Ltd

'Me' In Conflict, The © Pat Marsh
Meet Sam, aged 14 © John Grooms

No-one © Pat Marsh
Not Knowing Anyone, Marjorie Dobson © Stainer and Bell Ltd
Not That Easy © Geoffrey Herbert

O God, Put My Broken Pieces Together © Romeo L del Rosario
On a Diagnosis of Asperger's Syndrome © David Coleman
On My Own © Matthew Everitt
Other Side of Me, The © Pat Marsh

Prayer in Memory of Two Children Killed in a Road Tragedy © Christopher Bradnock
Prayer of Intercession for Safety on Our Roads © RoadPeace
Prayers for Road Victims and Their Families © RoadPeace

Rosa, an HIV+ Mozambican © Karen and Bill Butt

Safety © Roger Grainger
Separation or Divorce © Bernard Thorogood
Shoe Laces © Pat Marsh
Snowbound © Colin Ferguson
Soaring Wings and Strengthened Dreams (1) © Frances Biseker;
The Baptist Unjon of Great Britain; Women's Network of the Methodist Church;
Keri Wehlander (Canada)
Soaring Wings and Strengthened Dreams, (2) Keri Wehlander © United Church
Publishing House, United Church of Canada
Something to do with Fire © Cecily Taylor
Spiral Staircase © Margaret Alford
Still Life © Roger Grainger
Survival © Cecily Taylor

Tears © N Stevenson
Tenderness and Violence, Andrew Pratt © Stainer and Bell Ltd
Time © N Stevenson
Tom's Problem © John Grooms
Trust © Roger Grainger

What am I Waiting For? © Roger Grainger
When Parents Separate © Bernard Thorogood

You Disturb Me © Pat Marsh

Resourceful and Resilient

GCSEs Don't Come Into It © Mencap
God of the Emmaus Road © Geoffrey Duncan

Interview with Anne Begg MP, An © John Grooms
Invitation © Jean Palmer

Litany for Understanding and Infinite Love, A © Geoffrey Duncan
Living on the Edge of Communities © Rachel Lampard and Jennie Richmond,
formerly Catholic Housing Aid Society now Housing Justice

Master Furniture Maker © Ian Sanderson
Mature Women © Myrtle Walker
My Dream is to Learn Computer Skills © Traidcraft
My Friend Marty © Cecily Taylor

One Day at Emmaus © Emmaus UK
Ordinary People: Ordinary Moments © T Pradeep

Rocky Road, The © Ruth Patil

Smile is Something Special, The © Mencap
St Mary's – A Life-giving Source © Traidcraft

Taking A Chance © Jamie McCoy, Crisis Changing Lives

Undervalued – All in a Day's Work © Y Mochyn Daear
Useful Member of Her Community, A © Geoffrey Duncan

A Sri Lankan Journey

Sri Lankan Journey, A © Diane D'Souza

Reflections on Memories and Bereavement

After the Accident © Cecily Taylor
Afterwards (1) © Cecily Taylor
Afterwards (2) © Cecily Taylor
And Now You're Gone © Paul Taylor

Be Comforted in Your Grief © Richard Becher
Bereavement © Bernard Thorogood
Brokeness © Pat Marsh

Change © Giles Harcourt
Chapel, The © Roger Grainger
Child Grieving © Rosemary Parrott
Come Holy Spirit © Wendy Whitehead

Death in the Family, A © Bernard Thorogood

Epitaph to my Parents, An © Celia Snaith
Expectancy © Anthea Dove

Graveyard Dance © Hugh McKee

I Long to Grieve with All My Heart, Andrew Pratt © Stainer and Bell Ltd
In Bereavement © Jenny Dann
In Each Moment's Quiet Rememb'ring © Jan Berry

Last Time, The © Cecily Taylor
Lord, You Know Me Better Than I Know Myself © Richard Becher

Mass of Candles, A © David Bunney
Matthew 25 © Paul Friett
Moribund © Kim Fabricius
Mountain Symbol Will Rise, A © Eleanor Milardo
My Dead Sisters © Robert Fox

Nunc Dimittis © Pat Marsh from Bubbles and Rainbows and Butterfly Wings

One Year On © Rosemary Parrott

Prayer Service to Celebrate a Life for Women © Eleanor Milardo
Prayer Service to Celebrate a Life for Men © Eleanor Milardo

Reaching Out © Geoffrey Herbert Release © Pat Marsh
Release © Pat Marsh

Shining Like A Star © Richard Becher
Son © Elizabeth Cambridge
Symbols © Derek Webster

Tears © Cecily Taylor
To Ashley © Kevin Paul Woodbridge
Today is Our Hannah's Birthday © Kim Fabricius

Unusual Memorial Service, An © Jenny Dann and Denis Smith

Widow © Derek Webster

Travel Towards the Dawn

Blessing A, Christine Cargill © In God's Image Vol 20 No 4 December 2001, Journal of Asian Women's Resource Centre for Culture and Theology. Permission Sought.

Christian Ministry, A © Thomas Morton-Johns and John Tiernan, Prisons Week Committee
Collective Blessing, A, Source Unknown
Come to Us, Colleen Geyer © In God's Image Vol 20 No 4 December 2001, Journal of Asian Women's Resource Centre for Culture and Theology. Permission Sought.
Comforter, Marjorie Dobson © Stainer and Bell Ltd
Counsellor, The © Wendy Whitehead
Creed from An Urban Community in Britain, A, Source Unknown

Deep Community © John Ll Humphreys
Dreamer at Prayer © Wendy Whitehead

Family © Elizabeth Cambridge
Forgiveness for Walking on the Other Side of the Road © Clive Bates

Gay Children © Elizabeth Cambridge
God's Delight © Gillian Collins. First published in Magnet, issue number 63, Autumn 2003, the journal of the Women's Network of The Methodist Church.

Acknowledgements and Sources

Healing Hands © Wendy Whitehead
Hymn to Celebrate Ten Years of Women's Ordination © June Boyce-Tillman

I Don't Really Comprehend, Andrew Pratt © Stainer and Bell Ltd
I Sing a Song of the Woman's Voice © W L Wallace
I Stood Afar © Jill Fuller, The Leprosy Mission
If I Had the Power © Hannah Warwicker
Into The Light © Rosemary Parrott

Let his Dawn Light New Horizons, Marjorie Dobson © Stainer and Bell Ltd
Letting Go © Elizabeth Cambridge
Let Us Dream © Bangalore Initiative for Peace
Life is Getting Better © Jennifer Earthy
Little Lower Than God, A © John Ll Humphreys
Living With HIV and AIDS © London Ecumenical Aids Trust
Looking Forward © Elizabeth Cambridge
Lost Child Returns, The © Richard Becher

My Boy © St George's Crypt, Leeds, UK

Never Full Grown © Wendy Ross-Barker
None Out-ranks Another, Andrew Pratt © Stainer and Bell Ltd

On the Other Side © Pat Marsh
On the Road to Calvary © Colin Ferguson

People Who Continue to Care © Wendy Whitehead
Prayer Card © Elizabeth Cambridge
Prayer for Carers, A © Jenny Dann
Prayers for My Two Children Who are Both Gay © Elizabeth Cambridge

Red the Ribbon © David Mowbray

Tapestry © Denise Bennett
Thanksgiving for Care-workers, A © Wendy Whitehead

Unnamed Woman, An © Clare McBeath and Jill Thornton

Waiting on the Sofa © Jean Rahman Dalrymple
When I Pray to You for Help © W L Wallace

You and Me © C M Kao

Resources

It is good to have contributions from people involved with the following organisations. I am very grateful to the people in the various organisations who have assisted me with contributions from their members and friends.

Afrinspire
22 Melvin Way
Histon
Cambridge
CB4 9HY

Alzheimer's
Living with Dementia
11 – 15 Dix's Field
Exeter
EX1 1QA

Bible Society
Stonehill Green
Westlea
Swindon
SN5 7DG
www.biblesociety.org.uk

Campaign Against Arms Trade
11 Goodwin Street
London
N4 3HQ
www.caat.org.uk

CAFOD
Romero Close
London
SW9 9TY

Christian Aid
P O Box 100
London
SRE1 7RJ
www.christianaid.org.uk

Crisis
64 Commercial Street
London
E1 6LT
www.crisis.org.uk

Ecumenical Forum of European Christian Women
Anne Lambkin
6 Hangerfield Close
Yateley
Hants
GU46 6HR

Emmaus UK
48 Kingston Street
Cambridge
CB1 2NU
www.emmaus.org.uk

Find Your Feet
Unit 316
Bon Marche Centre
241 – 251 Ferndale road
London SW9 8BJ

In God's Image
Asian Women's Resource Centre
for Culture and Theology (AWRC)
119c – Batu 13½
Jalan Kelang Lama
58000 Kuala Lumpur
Malaysia

Jesuit Refugee Service
112 Thornbury Road
Osterley
Middlesex
TW7 4NN
www.jrsuk.net
www.jrseurope.org

John Grooms
50 Scrutton Street
London EC2A 4XQ
www.johngrooms.org.uk

Leprosy Mission
Goldhay Way
Orton Goldhay
Peterborough
PE2 5GZ
www.leprosymission.org.uk

London Ecumenical AIDS Trust
St Paul's Church
Lorrimer Square
London
SE17 3QU
www.leat.org.uk

Medical Aid for Iraqi Children
26 Old Brompton Road
London
SW7 3DL
www.maic.org.uk

Mencap
123 Golden Lane
London
EC1Y 0RJ
www.mencap.org.uk

Mildmay Mission Hospital
Hackney Road
London
E2 7NA
www.mildmay.org.uk

Multiple Sclerosis Society
Harris Bergman
M S Society
12 – 14 Ansell Street
London
W8 5TR
www.mssociety.org.uk

Nightstop
45A Otley Road
Shipley
BD18 3PY
www.nightstop-uk.org

Pestalozzi Children's Village trust
Sedlescombe
Battle
East Sussex
TN33 0RR
www.pestalozzi.org.uk

Prisons Week
P O Box 2733
Lichfield
Staffs
WS13 6GZ

RoadPeace
P O Box 2579
London
NW10 3PW
www.roadpeace.org

Stainer and Bell Ltd
P O Box 110
Victoria House
123 Gruneisen Road
Finchley
London
N3 1DZ

Traidcraft
Kingsway North
Gateshead
www.traidcraft.org.uk/giving matters
www.traidcraftshop.co.uk